W9-BRX-937

GUINEA PIGS

Their Care and Breeding
Patricia Hutchinson

Series Editor
Dennis Kelsey-Wood

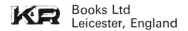 Books Ltd
Leicester, England

© K & R Books Ltd

All rights reserved. No part of this publication may be reproduced, stored in any retrieval system, or transmitted, in any form or by any means without the prior permission in writing of the publishers.

First published 1978
by K & R Books Ltd,
Leicester, England

ISBN 0 903264 21 8

Cover: A Self-Golden Boar owned by Mr. David Oulton.

Typeset by Albert Frost & Sons Ltd
Printed in Great Britain by
Colorgraphic Ltd, Leicester

Contents

Introduction

For many years I kept guinea pigs as pets and was completely unaware that they were anything other than pretty little pets often kept by children. I first saw a pure bred guinea pig at a local horse show where there were various sideshows, one of which was for rabbits and cavies. I did not at first recognise them as guinea pigs, they were so different to my own small pet. Wire pens with sawdust and hay in them were set out on tables and in each pen was a single animal. There were different breeds, colours, and markings whilst the shape of the heads, bodies, and even the size of some of the breeds left me amazed that I had never seen or heard about these animals before. I decided then and there that I wanted to enter this world of the cavy and see what it was all about.

I soon learnt that the cavy was far more than a pretty cross-bred pet. People from all walks of life devoted much of their time and energy to breeding and developing different varieties of cavies to produce the finest in the world. As Britain is famous for her bloodstock in horses, cattle, dogs, and other livestock, so also are Britain's cavies the finest, and they are exported to other countries to set up new breeding lines and improve established ones.

The following of the Cavy Fancy is very great and shows are held in all parts of the country, the two largest and most important being held annually in London, the London Championship Show, and Doncaster. The one which is equal to what Crufts is to the dog world is that put on by the Bradford Small Livestock Society held at Doncaster in the Grandstand on the racecourse. Visitors from America and the Continent regularly go to view the livestock and buy animals.

In these days of increasing pressures, worries, and tensions, to have an absorbing hobby is the best therapy for anyone.

To be able to appreciate and marvel at nature and the intelligence and ordered life of these small animals, to mix with others of similar interest at shows and meetings, or to just talk generally about them can be a relaxation. For youngsters it can teach them the meaning of responsibility to those dependent upon them.

Cavy keeping in the following chapters will be made clearer as we look into the requirements, the habits, and even into the private life of these fascinating little animals.

Patricia Hutchinson
Oxton, Birkenhead 1977

CHAPTER ONE

Housing

Cavies need adequate protection from variable weather, and outdoor accommodation is not suitable for breeding cavies for showing, or even those kept solely as pets. The ideal place to put your hutches, or pens as they are called, is a roomy wooden shed with windows that can be opened or shut according to the weather. A brick built outhouse or a garage can be used, but there should be adequate window space to provide full daylight and ventilation. A wire door should be made so that the entry of cats, dogs, mice, rats, or birds is prevented when the main door is open during the warmer months of the year. Some care should be taken when using a garage if a car is likely to be in and out as fumes from the exhaust could prove lethal.

Sheds, as well as having opening windows and a wire door, should have ventilation holes high up in the eaves to allow the warm humid air to escape and fresh air to come in. This is particularly necessary in the colder months when the wire door cannot be used and the windows cannot be fully opened. Holes can be drilled into the wood with a large size bit and small mesh wire can be placed over the outside to prevent the entry of mice. If desired, a sliding plastic grille which can be closed or opened according to the direction or strength of the wind can be placed over the inside holes.

The advantage of having your stock under cover is that it makes looking after them a much more comfortable task for yourself whilst good protection from draughts and damp is provided for the cavies.

Whilst cavies do not need elaborate pens, they should be constructed so that they give the maximum protection from draughts which means that doors should be well made and fit closely and joints should be closed and without gaps between them. This particularly applies to the floors and therefore use wood that will not shrink and create gaps in which the cavy could break its legs.

As a general guide, one cavy requires 1860 sqcm (2 sqft) of floor space, and this is an ideal area in which a pregnant sow can have her litter and rear her young to weaning age. Cavies running together should have 930 sqcm (1 sqft) of floor space each. Provided that the pens are not less than 50 cm (20 in) in depth from front to back and 40 cm (15 in) high, the length can be adjusted to provide the amount of floor space required. Cavies need quite a lot of exercise room, they are far more active than is generally supposed. Unfortunately many pet shops sell pens far too small for cavies or will recommend quite unsuitable metal cages. Cavies housed in pens with plenty of room will grow better, eat better, and be far happier and much more interesting animals.

Doors should open downwards from the top so that they will lie down flat when the pen is opened and not get in your way. Small 1·5 cm ($\frac{1}{2}$ in) mesh netting should be used, larger mesh being unsatisfactory as cavies can poke their noses through and chew the wire, cats can get their claws through, and mice can gain entry. The stronger wire is really the most satisfactory, being longer lasting and giving a stronger finish to the door.

It is absolutely essential that "drop-boards" are fitted to the front of the pens to prevent the cavies from falling out when the doors are opened, as well as to keep the bedding in. The boards can be made of hardboard or thin plywood and should be about 10 cm (4 in) to 13 cm (5 in) deep. Slots should be cut into each side of the pen for them to slide into so that the boards can be removed for cleaning. An easy way of making the slots is to use a piece of the groove side of tongue and groove board and nail it to each side of the pen just inside the door, allowing space for the door to shut. Offcuts of hardboard are ideal and cheap and they can be replaced periodically as necessary.

Provided that your shed is draught free there is no need to provide separate compartments for sleeping, but it is a good practice to place pieces of plastic sheeting over part of the

Tiered Hutches.

doors, say about a quarter to one third, for some protection when the windows or doors are open. The cavies can hide behind this as they do seem to like a little privacy. These pieces of plastic sheet can be simply taped onto the pens and are easily removed when the weather is particularly hot, or replaced during inclement weather.

Pens can be made with a division up the middle and a space between the doors, so that one can be used as either a single pen or made into two separate pens by sliding a sheet of plywood between. This is particularly useful when you need a number of pens in which sows can have their litters.

Each set of pens can be stacked one on top of the other, but the first row should be set up off the floor by about 30 cm (12 in) to allow air to circulate, and in between each set there should be at least 5 cm (2 in) of space for air circulation and to keep the bottoms of the pens dry. Do not stack your pens so high that you cannot see or reach easily into them—arrange your shed to cater for your own comfort as well as the animals'.

Protection can be given to the wooden floors by lining the pens with newspaper and then placing a good layer of sawdust or shavings on this together with some hay for bedding, the newspaper makes it much easier for cleaning as it can simply be pulled out and disposed of together with the litter and replaced by fresh newspaper and litter. Cavies should be cleaned out at least once a week and every so often the pens scrubbed with hot water and common soda or a disinfectant. Allow the pens to dry thoroughly before reusing and they will last for years.

There is no need to treat the insides of the pens with anything, simply leave the wood plain but clean. The outsides can be treated for appearances sake if required, but as they are not open to the elements this is not a necessity. However, if you wish to paint the outside wood be sure that no part can be reached by a cavy and that all trace of smell has gone before cavies are put in them.

In warm weather cavies can be run in wire pens on the lawn, but a well constructed cage should be made with a compartment into which they can shelter in the event of rain or cold weather. The compartment is necessary in hot weather too as cavies can suffer heat exhaustion and must have shade from the hot sun. They should not on any account be left out overnight but must be returned to their inside pens as dampness is one thing that a cavy cannot tolerate. Generally breeders do not run their stock outside and indeed unless the animals have become accustomed to this they will just sit in a corner of the cage. However, pet cavies can provide interest for young members of the family and indeed the older ones too, but the outdoor cage must be covered not only on the sides but also on the top with 1·5 cm ($\frac{1}{2}$ in) wire mesh so that there is no chance of cats, dogs, or vermin getting into them with very disastrous results.

As long as you have your first set of pens ready for your initial purchase of cavies you can then plan your remaining space to its best advantage with pens as simple as you wish or as elaborate as you fancy, but the important thing to remember is that the cavy must have dry, draught free quarters with good air circulation.

There is no need for heating to be installed as the cavy can withstand quite low temperatures provided that it has plenty of hay and the atmosphere is dry, although if you intend to breed during the winter months heating can be of great help. Many breeders in the colder parts of the country do have heating for the extremely cold weather, or if their area is damp and condensation occurs heating is very beneficial.

In my own shed I have electric greenhouse heaters installed on a thermostatic control which will just lift the temperature in the very cold weather. I use these when litters are due and they also make the shed a more comfortable place when I wish to spend some time in there examining stock and getting it ready for showing. Heat is also useful when I have bathed a cavy as I can ensure that the temperature is raised so that the animal will not catch a cold when I return it to its pen after being dried in the house. These heaters are the long, tubular, fully enclosed electric type. Heating should be only by this form of fully enclosed heater with no fire risk. Oil lamps, paraffin (kerosene) heaters, and open electric fires should never be taken into the caviary, for apart from the danger of fumes from the paraffin (kerosene), the danger of fire is ominous.

Electric lighting is very essential and the small initial outlay will be well justified during the darker months.

CHAPTER TWO

Feeding

Feeding the cavy is quite a simple matter as long as you remember the following basic principles:

1. It must have vitamin C every day
2. It must have hay every day
3. It must have corn every day
4. It must have water every day
5. It should never be fed frosted food, stale food, or anything that is musty, rotten or mouldy.

These points will be explained in the following pages and show the wide variety of foods that can be given.

Vitamin C is a most important thing to remember for the cavy has a requirement very uncommon in the animal world in that it cannot live without vitamin C being provided in the diet. It shares this requirement with man, the ape family, and very few other creatures. Other animals like the rabbits and dogs do not need to have this supplied to them as they can manufacture their own requirements.

Vitamin C is found in greenfoods, fruit, and roots such as fresh beetroot and carrots although the content in greens is much higher. During the winter when greens are not readily available beetroot and carrots retain this vitamin very well. An adult cavy requires about 10 mg of vitamin C a day and a pregnant sow 20 mg per day. As an adult cavy will usually eat between 113 grams ($\frac{1}{4}$ lb) to 226 grams ($\frac{1}{2}$ lb) of roots or even more, then as the beetroot and carrots have about 3 mg of vitamin C per ounce this should provide enough for their needs. The requirements of a pregnant sow are higher and this is dealt with in the breeding section. During the latter part of the winter root vegetables are starting to deteriorate and if they are not hard and crisp the vitamin C content will have deteriorated, so if fresh greens are available these should be included in the diet. However, not everybody is situated so that they can obtain greens and it is therefore a good idea to obtain "Redoxon" effervescent vitamin C tablets from the chemist (pharmacist) and put some into the drinking water or in the water you use to make up any mashes you may feed to the cavies. Each tablet is 1 gram which is sufficient for 100 cavies at 10 mg per cavy, so if you have only a small stud you need only use a small piece of tablet each day, or just on the days you cannot supply sufficient greens.

Cauliflower trimmings are very much liked by cavies and are probably their favourite of the vegetable greens available. Your local greengrocer or market trader will usually save them for you, but do not use them if they are wilting, going yellow, or marked with black blotches; they should be crisp and fresh. Sometimes greengrocers will throw out very large carrots or split ones which you can use, but on no account use those going soft or mouldy as this would cause severe tummy upsets. If you have a large number of animals a local fruit and vegetable wholesaler will sell you a bag of carrots or beetroot at wholesale price. These usually come in 10 Kg (22 lb) or 13 Kg (28 lb) bags, but these are usually washed before being bagged so buy only what you can use in a week as washed roots go off quite quickly. If you can obtain unwashed vegetables these will last much longer, but you must wash the vegetables yourself before feeding them. Beetroots are not usually very dirty and as the cavy leaves the outer skin anyway it is not essential that these be washed. They like beetroots cut into quarters so that they can eat the fleshy part easily whilst carrots are enjoyed if the top crown and the bottoms are cut off and the carrots then split up the middle, preferably into four.

A list of foods that can be fed in the winter and in the summer can be found at the end of this chapter, including details of some of the food values.

Summer feeding can consist of fresh grass which is the cavy's most natural and favourite food. Fresh grass clippings or mowings are not really very satisfactory and cavies are not particularly fond of short mown grass. Cuttings can be particularly dangerous if left to become hot, which they do in a very short time, for if fed they will cause severe scouring and even death. If you do feed them, clear away any that are not eaten, do not leave them in the pen to become hot and yellow and perhaps be eaten later. The longer grass from the fields is much preferred. If you live in an area where it is not possible to supply fresh grass every day and you just gather some from the local park or play field, do be careful that it has not been sprayed with weed killer or any pesticide and also that it is not where dogs could have contaminated it. Cavies do not usually suffer from worms but they can be infected by eating grass that is contaminated.

The summer feeding can be a most interesting time. If you cannot gather grass, local gardeners will often let you have greens and trimmings whilst some of the weeds that grow in gardens can be used for feeding, but ensure they have not been sprayed with chemicals of any kind. If you have a garden you can grow many of the items mentioned later for feeding your stock. A trip into the country can provide extra interest when taking a bag for collecting various plants and herbs and finding succulent grass to take back to the caviary.

When feeding grass for the first time after a long winter, or if the animals are not used to it on a regular basis, introduce this and any herbs slowly to enable the animals' stomachs to become used to the change in the diet. Do not throw a huge pile in for the first feed, tempting though it is to watch them try to eat it as fast as they can, just give a handful or so at a time until they can be fed completely on grass, hay and corn in the summer.

Hay: The next important requirement is hay, and without this form of food the cavy cannot digest what it has eaten. Hay also provides an unknown factor, without which the cavy would develop digestion troubles, chew its own hair and that of its companions, and it would not develop or grow. Never skimp on feeding hay and make sure that it is the best you can buy with no sign of mould or dust. The smell alone will tell you whether it is good or bad hay. Cavies prefer the soft meadow hay to the harder coarser type, but this can be used if soft hay is not available. Hay made early when the seed is still intact is the best but as so much depends on the weather and when it can be gathered, then as long as it is well made and has not been lying around, when it has a bleached and faded look about it, then it will provide many of the things needed by your cavy to keep fit and well. Hay also provides a better source of warmth as bedding in the winter than straw, but if you cannot always obtain good hay then good clean oat straw contains some feeding value and is better than really bad hay. Barley straw should not be used as the spines off the barley can cause injury. Wheat straw serves no beneficial purpose but is sometimes used to bed light coloured cavies to prevent the staining of their coats when they are show pigs. There is, however, no substitute for good hay.

If you can buy a bale direct from a farmer you will probably obtain it cheaper than from a dealer and also the farmer will be likely to let you choose your own. Do not buy anything but the best. Poor hay can be dangerous particularly if it has white mould or smells damp, and therefore do not use any part that is affected, and if it has thistles in it pull them out before feeding. Lots of breeding troubles can result from poor quality hay. It is a valuable source of protein, carbohydrates, and minerals, and also serves the purpose of keeping the cavy busy nibbling away. Of course in the summer the supply can be cut down, as they will not need it so much for bedding, but they still require enough to eat.

A word of caution though, new made hay should not be used, no matter what you may be told. Hay must have a period of ''sweating out'' after it has been baled and stacked. Farmers do not feed new made hay to their stock nor should it be used for cavies or it could cause digestion disorders. It should ideally be 6 months old, but it can be used at 4/5 months old.

Corn: Sometimes called concentrates. This is necessary as a source of body building and energy giving material as well as certain vitamins and minerals. A variety of these cereals includes oats, barley, wheat, flaked maize, bran which is a by-product of wheat, and manufactured rabbit pellets.

The most popular cereal is oats that have been crushed, as a cavy cannot eat whole oats, and many farmers or pet shops sell these ready crushed. They should just have the outer skins split so that the oat is not ground up into a powder but adheres to the skin. If they have been crushed until the kernel is a powder they are best fed mixed with some bran—two parts oats to one part bran—and dampened into a mash with a little water, otherwise the cavies will be rather wasteful with this form of food. However, experience comes with practice and you will soon know good oats from bad, as you will know good hay from bad.

When oats are not available barley can be used, but again this must be crushed. It is rather more heating than oats, so care has to be taken not to feed it quite so freely. Lighter coloured cavies tend to overheat more quickly than the darker varieties. When a cavy overheats the hair comes out of the centre of the back and it is sometimes referred to as "broken backed". The remedy is to feed less heating food. Wheat can be used but is expensive, and is also rather heating, and as bran has more food value in it than the wheat bran is the better buy. Flaked maize, which looks like corn-flakes, is very high in calories and is also very fattening. This is not recommended for feeding to pregnant sows, but rather to young growing stock, and even then it should only be fed very sparingly.

There are various mixes that can be used, but the most usual one is the 3 :2 :1 mix, this is three parts of good bran, two parts middlings (this is wheat meal) and one part oatmeal, the resulting mixture being fed as damp mash. There is the 2 :1 mix mentioned previously, and many others with all kinds of ingredients. Rabbit pellets are sometimes used, they are soaked overnight in just enough water to make them crumbly and then dried off with bran into a mash. This is quite good for growing youngsters but I have found it makes breeding sows inclined to become too fat and thus not breed well.

Dry mixes are favoured by some and such things as oats, barley, flaked maize and rabbit pellets are mixed together and fed dry. I, however, think that this is rather an expensive and wasteful method as the cavy becomes very selective and sorts out what it likes, often picking out the pellets and dropping them in the litter and wasting the rest, which in view of the rising world prices of grains is something that is to be avoided.

The concentrate part of my cavies' diet, which I have been using for years, is very simple, economical, and really enjoyed by the animals. It is a plain bran mash in the morning made up of bran dampened slightly with water to make a crumbly mash. Once or twice a week if I have some brown bread, I soak this in water, squeeze it out as dry as possible and mix it in with the bran just as a change. This mash is fed quite liberally and in addition to this they always have a pot of crushed oats in the pen which I top up last thing at night when feeding the other parts of their diet. In the summer, provided that they are getting grass twice a day, they have a bran mash only two or three times a week. Roots, greens, and hay provide the rest of the vitamins and minerals that are required, and there is no need for additives such as cod liver oil or vitamin supplements, and in fact the addition could do more harm than good.

Corn and mash should be fed in heavy earthenware pots, usually obtainable from pet shops. The pots used for rabbits are ideal, but lightweight ones will be easily tipped up and the contents become wasted. The cavy likes to put its front feet on the rim of the pot when feeding, and unless the dish is heavy it will tip up. Boars will often pick a pot up and tip the contents out and fling the pot upside down, this is probably part of trying to impress sows, but it can be very annoying so a good heavy pot will mean less wastage.

The pots should be kept really clean. They should be soaked in detergent and warm water until any food or dirt will come off, and they should then be well rinsed and left to drain. This should be done at least once a week, and more often in the summer because food allowed to go sour or mouldy particles on the inside of the pots are a source of infection and stomach disorders. If you wish to carry out a form of sterilising and disinfecting your pots, then the addition of some Vanodine 18 to your last rinsing water will accomplish this.

Just common-sense and cleanliness will keep your cavy a fit and healthy animal and make your hobby a much more enjoyable one.

Water: Amongst a number of misconceptions about the cavy is the one that it does not need water. This is almost as bad as the old chestnut about their eyes dropping out if you pick them up by their tails! Of course they need water and will drink it readily and in quite large quantities, particularly in the summer or when nursing youngsters. Some breeders say they can live without it, and undoubtedly they can but there is a difference between existing and living, and there is a difference between an unfit cavy and a fit one. Perfect fitness counts very much when showing cavies, and one way of achieving this is to supply all of its basic needs. An argument put forward is that if sufficient greens are fed water is not necessary, but do not be talked out of giving water. It is a little more trouble keeping the water bottles clean, but the results will be well worth the extra trouble. Water is best given to cavies by way of water bottles that have a metal tube, do not use a glass tube as they can crack this in a moment. The bottle, readily available from pet shops, is filled with water, turned upside down, and attached to the wire part of the door by means of two hooks and an elastic band, the bottle, of course, on the outside of the wire and the metal tube going through for the cavy to take water. They require cleaning now and again and this is easily done by means of a bristle bottle brush obtainable from most stores, whilst the metal tubes can be cleaned by twisting three or four pipe cleaners together and pushing these up the tube immersed in water, again Vanodine 18 can be used in the final rinsing water. Water supplied in pots is unsatisfactory because cavies will sit in it and soil or spill it and their pens become wet and damp.

Unfresh or Mouldy Food: Although the cavy is a healthy little animal with the correct management, it can nonetheless soon have an upset stomach if fed the wrong food. Anything which is not fresh, is going yellow, soft, or rotten should be avoided. If you wish to make up a corn mix it is advisable that you buy your own ingredients and make certain that they are not mouldy or contaminated with mouse or rat droppings. It is a good precaution to have a look at any corn you contemplate buying, and the ingredients should smell wholesome. Rabbit pellets should be hard and firm and not crumble when one is squeezed between the fingers. Bran should not be adhering to itself in lumps and preferably should be broad flaked. By making up your own mix rather than buying it ready made you will know that it is as fresh as possible. Do not buy a larger quantity than you can use in a few weeks as corn that has been crushed will not keep, particularly if stored in a damp atmosphere.

Greenfoods and roots should be fresh and crisp. Roots do tend to go off towards the months of March and April because of long storage, and therefore pick out carefully any that are going black, soft, or mouldy. Frosted food should never be fed until every trace of frost has gone from it, so be sure to store your supplies where they will be well protected and not become frosted.

You cannot feed cavies according to weights and measures, you must feed according to appetite. A pen of young growing cavies can eat an enormous amount of food—it is almost impossible to overfeed youngsters. Always feed so that there is some left over, if they clear up everything then it is not enough so feed more, particularly to intended show stock. Care, however, must be shown with breeding stock for you do not want them to become fat. They tend to become sometimes overweight after their first litter and when they are fully grown, so if they are greedy keep the corn allowance to a minimum but ensure plenty of greens, roots and hay.

The number of times you feed your stock will depend on your own particular situation. Ideally they should be fed in the morning and in the evening, although a few titbits given mid-day do not go amiss. The main meal should be given at night as this is when cavies eat most of their food. If they are given a mash, some greens or roots, and hay at the morning feed, ensure that their supply of hay is sufficient to last until evening. It can then be replenished when the bulk of the food is fed to them. Try to keep a regular pattern of feeding as cavies can become quite agitated when a meal is late or missed, and the noise they make when you go into the caviary will tell you what they think.

When you buy cavies always ask the breeder what they have been fed on and try to keep as near to this as possible until they settle down, as cavies do not change their eating habits readily. Do not think that if they are hungry enough they will eat, they very often will not and this combined with the change of ownership could cause stress and some weight loss. Gradually you can change them to your own methods, and young stock are always quicker to adapt than older ones.

LIST OF ROOT AND VEGETABLES for winter feeding

Beetroot (Red Globe type) : This is the best root and the favourite one too as the cavy's choice. It is a real body builder and conditioner, but do not feed much of the leafy tops as they contain too much oxalic acid. The food content of beetroot is very high in relation to other roots and it contains calcium, iron, and other elements, with Vitamin C content about 3 mg per ounce.

Carrots: These are wholesome and easily digestible, very rich in vitamins, sugar, and oil, and have a high food value. They contain calcium and iron, and the Vitamin C content is about the same as beetroot.

Swedes and Turnips: Not a very high food value as they are mostly made up of water and fibre and soon go dry and fibrous. Vitamin C content is 7 mg per ounce, but this deteriorates quickly.

Mangel-Wurzels: These must not be fed until after February as when they are freshly harvested they have a very high oxalic acid content. They have to be stored in a clamp or hog to ripen when the oxalates become insoluble, they should still be used with caution as they have a purgative action and pregnant sows should never be fed on them. Lighter coloured cavies are sometimes fed on these because they do not stain the fur for showing. Very low Vitamin C content.

Chicory: The Witloof Chicory is the type usually grown for feeding to cavies. A very good conditioner, liked by cavies and easy to grow.

Cauliflowers: The trimming of the outside leaves are enjoyed by cavies but they will not eat the white crown of this plant. Be sure the trimmings are clean and fresh looking.

Sprout Tops, Spring Cabbage and Broccoli (White or Purple) : Cavies will not eat sprouts but the tops of the plants will be eaten and when the plant is finished the thick stalks can be slit and the cavies will eat the white flesh inside. They do not like white cabbage, only the green leaves. Spring Cabbage will be eaten if nothing else is available but it is not cne of their favourite foods. Broccoli leaves from the White or Purple Sprouting varieties is enjoyed very much. The Vitamin C contents of all the cabbage family is very high at around 17/20 mg per ounce.

Spinach: Not all cavies will eat this but it adds variety to the diet and can be used as a treat. Vitamin C content about 17/20 mg per ounce.

Celery: The tops and outside stalks make a welcome change, but should be thoroughly washed before feeding and used only as a treat. About 2 mg Vitamin C per ounce.

Apple: Cavies usually like these and will eat them quite readily. Use as a treat. Only 1 mg per ounce Vitamin C content.

Watercress: Must be well washed and use only as a treat. The calcium content is extremely high.

WILD PLANTS FOR FEEDING

In the following, as well as giving the more popularly known name of the herbs and weeds that can be gathered, I have given the Universal or Latin name of the plant so that you can identify any plant you do not know by referring to a book on wild plants. If in any doubt about any plant, remember the old saying "IF IN DOUBT, LEAVE IT OUT"

When gathering greens, those growing under trees may not be palatable as some trees drop a sticky liquid from their leaves and blossoms which makes the grass and vegetation below bitter tasting. Do not gather any greens that have bird droppings on them as they could prove deadly.

Mix all the greens to give a balanced mixture as some plants are laxative and some astringent. Grass can be fed on its own, and indeed this is what they will go for before any other greenfood is touched. If only grass is available you could not have anything better, the weeds and herbs only add interest to the diet and make a pleasant change.

Do, however, be most careful that where you gather has not been treated by any chemical pesticide, weedkiller, or fertiliser.

20

Bramble *(Rubus fruticosus):* The leaves can be used for the treatment of scours but remove the thorny spine of the leaf first. Stock seem to eat them quite readily, especially the very young new shoots.

Coltsfoot *(Tussilago farfara):* The flowers of this plant are yellow and appear before the leaves in early March. Both can be used and are very safe foods. This plant was once used as a treatment for asthma and colds in humans.

Chickweed *(Stellaria media):* Although it is not readily eaten, it is one of the few edible plants that contains copper. Makes a change with other greens, but do not feed it in large quantities. A little is said to have cooling and soothing qualities. This plant is rather similar to Scarlet Pimpernel which is poisonous and, as the name suggests, has scarlet flowers whereas Chickweed has a white flower.

Clovers and Trefoils *(Trifolium pratense*, Red Clover*) (Trifolium repens*, White Clover*)* : Very nutritious and a good conditioner mixed well with other greens—do not feed in large quantities.

Trefoils *(Trifolium arvense*, Hare's Foot Trefoil and *Trifolium porcumbens*, Hop Trefoil) are miniature clovers. The Hare's Foot has a bushy pink/white flower and the Hop Trefoil a yellow hop shaped flower. Very nutritious plant much prized in grasses for making hay.

Dandelions *(Taraxacum officinale):* Appear very early, are of a laxative nature and increase the action of the kidneys, so just a little at a time.

Docks *(Rumex acetosa):* These are of an astringent nature and can be used with greens such as Dandelion. Do not, however, use too many. When the flower stalks begin to appear the acid content increases so from then on do not use. This plant is officially listed as poisonous for farm animals if eaten in quantity, but a little mixed with the cavy's other greens is beneficial; they seem to like its acid taste. Dock is usually the broadleaved or long curly leaved type, do not use the short sheep sorrel with a spear shaped leaf.

Grass: The best green food of all as previously mentioned. Stock thrive on this. Do not collect from grass verges of roads as exhaust fumes from traffic will have contaminated it, making it lethal.

Coltsfoot

Shepherds Purse

Yarrow

Dandelion.

Clover

SOME EDIBLE GREEN FOODS.

Foxglove

Lily of the Valley

Convolvulus

Deadly Nightshade.

Buttercup

SOME POISONOUS PLANTS.

Ground Elder *(Aegopodium podagraria):* Sometimes called Goutweed. This plant has a diuretic action, which means it increases the action of the kidneys. Do not use this once the flower stalks appear but it is quite safe to use before, mixed with grass and other greens. It appears very early in the spring and has tonic properties.

Groundsel *(Senecio vulgaris):* This is a laxative stimulating plant, valuable to birds and rabbits at moulting time. A little can be mixed daily with greens to improve the diet. However, this plant is often affected by white mould which would make it dangerous to feed to cavies, so examine the underside carefully.

Hawkweed *(Hieracium pilosella)* or Hawkbit, is a useful food quite safe and enjoyed.

Knapweed *(Centaurea scabiosa):* Sometimes known as Hardheads. The large leaves that grow around the base of the plant are appreciated, rather than the tough stalks. They appear very early in Spring and then again about August or September a fresh supply will appear.

Knotgrass *(Polygonum aviculare):* Has an acid content, so do not use large quantities. Watch that it is not affected by white fungus. It is a low growing, creeping plant so if gathered near roads it might need washing.

Mallow or Cheese Flower *(Malva sylvestris):* A very safe plant with no bad properties.

Nipplewort *(Lapsana communis):* Another safe plant and a valuable addition to the diet. The flowers are similar in colour and shape to the dandelion, only smaller. Rabbits love this plant.

Plantains *(Plantago media):* There are two types, the broad leaved which is usually called Plantain, and the long leaved variety called **Ribwort** *(Plantago lanceolata)*. Valuable source of vitamins and minerals that are not always found in other plants. Will not upset even the youngest stock.

Sow Thistle *(Sonchus arvensis):* Sometimes called Milk Thistle but not to be confused with poisonous Milk Weed, similar in name but nothing like Milk Thistle in appearance. Sow Thistle is a very good food for nursing sows. A favourite plant much sought after, but not as plentiful as it once was. Often found on old building sites and derelict ground. Can be affected by a white fungus, in which case do not use.

Shepherd's Purse *(Capsella bursa-pastoris):* Well known for its astringent qualities and used widely for treatment of scours. The entire plant can be fed, but wash soil off roots first. This is also often attacked by a white fungus and if so do not use.

Vetches *(Vicia sepium, Vicia cracca*, et al*):* A member of the pea family. Useful and valuable food that cavies like very much. Often sown with grass. Contains nitrogenic properties necessary for health and adds lustre to the fur of animals and the feathers of birds. All types of vetches are safe to use, but only when it has not been attacked by the white fungus.

Yarrow *(Achillea millefolium):* Sometimes called Milfoil, a graceful and feathery plant which emits an aromatic odour when crushed. Often sown with grasses because of its valuable tonic properties. Contains oil and is better fed when young and tender than when in flower. It sends up young shoots early in spring and again at the end of August.

POISONOUS PLANTS including some doubtful ones

Bracken *(Pteridium aquilinum):* This is dangerous as it contains an enzyme which destroys the vitamin B1 content in the tissues.

Buttercups *(Ranunculus family):* These are poisonous, although a few gathered in grass appear to do no harm, and it is sometimes unavoidable. Pick out as much as possible and do not gather grass that has very much mixed in with it. It is, however, harmless when dried in hay.

Bryony White *(Bryonia dioica):* Very poisonous, of different family to **Black Bryony** *(Tamus communis)* which is also very poisonous. Sometimes called Chilblain Berry.

Charlock *(Sinapis arvensis):* Usually seen growing amongst corn or farm crops. Poisonous in all its forms although it is a common belief that it is not poisonous until the seed pods have formed. This is not true.

Convolvulus *(Convolvulus arvensis)* or Bindwind, known to Gardeners as Devil's Guts.

Deadly Nightshade *(Atropa belladona):* From this plant

Atropine and Hyoscymine drugs are obtained.

Foxglove *(Digitalis purpurea):* The drug Digitalis is obtained from this.

Hellebore *(Helleborus foetidus):* Sometimes known as Stinking Hellebore. Contains narcotic poison.

Henbane *(Hyoscyamus niger):* Is a coarse plant which smells horrible. It remains poisonous when dried, but luckily quite an uncommon plant.

Horsetails *(Equisetum):* Sometimes called Marestails. A plant which is becoming very widespread in parts of the country and is poisonous even when dried. It is a very coarse and abrasive plant and not easily missed. It looks like a flue brush.

Hemlock *(Conium maculatum):* Whilst most poisonous plants contain poisons which when used in minute quantities medically can be beneficial, this plant has no useful part whatsoever and is most dangerous. It is similar to **Hedge Parsley** and is of the same family group and for this reason I have not listed the latter in the safe foods. It is so similar in appearance that it is best not touched, nor indeed should any of this plant family or its relative **Water Hemlock**

Lily of the Valley *(Convallaria majalis):* The source of one of the deadliest rat poisons.

Monkshood *(Aconitum Napellus):* The poison Aconite is derived from this plant.

Mayweeds *(Matricaria and Anthemis)* or Chamomile : All these daisy type plants are officially listed as poisonous, although some seem to think they are not.

Privet *(Ligustrum vulgare):* Horses have been known to die from eating this.

Scarlet Pimpernel *(Anagallis arvensis):* As previously mentioned, any of the Pimpernel family of plants should be avoided.

Ragwort *(Senecio jacobaea):* A very common large growing weed in pastures. It is dangerous to all animals and few will ever eat it. Because of its delayed action on the liver the death of an animal is not always attributed to it and it has been listed as safe to feed to small livestock in some literature. It is a most dangerous plant and retains its poisonous property when dried in hay, but because of its large size and yellow flowers it is usually noticed.

Spurges or Milkweed *(Euphorbia helioscopia): (*Not Milk Thistle as previously mentioned.) The blossoms and the leaves are the same green colour.

Toadflax *(Linaria vulgaris):* Looks like miniature snapdragons.

Wild Celery *(Apium graveolens):* Similar to the Hedge Parsley and Hemlock plants.

Wild Beaked Parsley *(Anthriscus sylvestris).*

White Fungus: Any plants afflicted by it are poisonous because it contains a poison called Ergot, any plant affected with fungus of any kind should be discarded.

All plants that grow from bulbs.

CHAPTER THREE

Breeding

The cavy is a member of the rodent family but it does not follow the normal rodent pattern with regard to bearing its young. It has a very long gestation period for so small an animal, 70 days being the usual time although births a few days before or after are not unusual. Because of this long gestation period the babies are born with their eyes open, fully furred, and able to run around almost immediately. Their stomachs are capable of taking the same food as adults and digesting it without any trouble. It is quite normal to see babies chewing small pieces of hay even before they are dry from birth. The sow can rear four babies, and even more in the summer, from her two milk glands, the babies seeming to wait their turn to be fed although a very tiny baby may be pushed away. Plenty of food for the sow and some bread and milk for the babies will help a large litter to be reared successfully, and provided they are well fed they will grow quite normally once they get past weaning age and will not be stunted as is sometimes supposed. Often babies can be successfully fostered to another nursing sow as will be discussed later in this chapter.

Young sows can be bred from at about 5 months of age provided they are fit and well. Some breeds vary on the recommended age but they should not be left too long before being bred from as a sow that has not had a litter by the time she is 10 months old is more likely to have trouble due to her bones and ligaments being less supple and she may prove difficult to mate.

Young boars, although they will behave rather precociously from as young as 4 weeks of age, are not usually potent until about 10 weeks but different breeds vary. It does no harm to give a young boar a sow and in fact it will stop him fretting on his own. When he is about 6 months old he is usually large enough to manage quite well with more sows.

Whilst four or five sows can be run with one boar you must NEVER have more than one boar in the breeding pen as they would kill one another even if they have been brought up together. Once they have sight and smell of sows they must never again be put with another boar.

The sow comes into season approximately every sixteen days. Matings are not often seen unless one spends a lot of time in the caviary, so it is not possible to always know just when a litter is due. However, there is always unusual activity in a pen where a sow is in season and if you see a boar chasing a sow with a lot of squealing and rushing about going on it is as well to make a note of the date and identify the particular sow. Have a look later to see if there is any sign of sperm around the vent which will indicate that a mating has taken place. If she does not come into season after 16 days or so, then it can be assumed that she is in pig and you can count 70 days from the date of the mating to establish when she should be due. Maiden sows usually mate the first time but some are a little difficult and may not mate immediately. Cavies are not as quick to breed as rabbits so it is not possible to plan your litters; some sows can take months before deciding to mate.

The unborn babies start to move inside the sow at about 42 days and this is called "quickening". At 50 days the movements are very definite and if the sow does not mind being handled manoeuvre her into a convenient part of the pen and place your hands along the sides slightly underneath her tummy, not pressing or squeezing, and you will shortly feel a very definite sharp movement. This examining is called palpating and if you palpate the sow each week from when she begins to become noticeably larger, then when you can feel these definite movements it can be assumed that this is about the fiftieth day and birth should take place 18/20 days hence. Before the birth the pelvic bone will start to open, usually 3/4 days before birth, but it can vary from 5/10 days to as little as an hour or two. The pelvic bone is the hard bony structure that can be felt just in front of the vent, and if the sow is quiet you can slide your hand under her tummy and

29

gently feel the two ends of the pelvic bone tightly shut. Near to birth it will gradually start to open and you will notice the difference quite plainly. Some bones open about 1 cm ($\frac{1}{2}$ in) to 2 cm ($\frac{3}{4}$ in) whilst others only open very slightly. With practice you will know when they are open and this will give you an idea as to when birth is due. If your sow is at all frightened however leave her alone, you will do more harm than good. Always when handling or lifting a pregnant sow ensure that the heavy mass of her tummy is adequately supported by your hand, both hands if necessary, as the extra weight of the babies, fluid, placenta and such can almost equal her own normal body weight. Apart from taking her out to clean her pen, the less she is actually lifted the better.

Some fanciers prefer leaving the pregnant sows in with the boar and letting them litter in the breeding pen together.

Group of various colours.

Another practice is to remove the pregnant sow from the main breeding pen and put her into a smaller pen some time before birth so that she can have her litter on her own, and yet another method is to have one boar with one sow and to remove the boar shortly before the sow is due to litter. Each method has its advantages and disadvantages which each fancier can evaluate according to circumstances.

The first method is adopted more frequently in large studs where room is limited or where one is breeding for the waster trade (research) but this method is not recommended to breeders who intend breeding show stock. There is higher mortality here due to babies being trampled upon by the adults. When the sow comes into season, which she does a few hours after giving birth, the babies can be scattered and trampled upon in the general rushing about and excitement that accompanies mating. This means that the sow will not only be nursing a litter but will also have the added strain of carrying another litter, which may be acceptable now and again if the sow has only one or two babies. This immediate mating is called a postpartum mating, but sows should not be treated as breeding machines and ideally should have a short rest between litters. Another factor to consider in this method of littering is that there will be other pregnant sows in the pen and they will lick and attend to the other sow's babies as they are born, which in turn causes them to become excited and start their own contractions which means that they will abort their litters. This can happen when they are only 4/5 weeks pregnant onwards and consequently there is the risk of not only losing a litter but the sow as well. Some baby sows can come into season very early, as early as 2/3 weeks of age, and it has been known for these young sows to mate with their father and become pregnant. This is very undesirable and not to be recommended to anyone. It is also very difficult to keep records if all the babies of several sows are mixed up as they do not stick to their own mothers but feed anywhere they can. This means that you could end up with one sow trying to feed all the babies. Nursing sows are very accommodating and will nurse anyone's babies.

The second method of removing the pregnant sow from the main breeding pen and putting her in a pen to have her babies on her own is the one I prefer and have found the most successful with hardly any loss of youngsters. However, I did find that this could cause some stress in an occasional sow due to being put into a strange pen without the company she had been used to, it could lead to the sow aborting her young 5/7 days from the date of removal from the main pen. When removing the sow I now also remove the boar and put them together in the new pen. I leave the boar with her for a few days until the pen has taken on a familiar smell which makes it her own. The boar can then be returned to the breeding pen and no stress has been caused to the sow in the transition from breeding to littering pen.

The third method of putting just one sow and one boar together is fine if you do not require the boar for any other sows and provided that the pen is large enough to ensure plenty of exercise for them both. The boar can be removed just before the sow is due to litter.

The number of babies born is determined by the sow, the boar merely fertilises the ova released by the sow, and litters of 1 to 4 are usual but litters of 5/10 have been recorded. Four babies is ideally plenty for a sow to rear but in the winter a litter of this size can be a bit of a strain and some help should be given, either by fostering the babies or feeding them.

Three litters a year is quite enough and a rest during the winter months does not go amiss. However, if a sow is in a good fit condition after rearing her litter and weaning them, she can be put back into the breeding pen. The danger of leaving sows too long is that they can become fat and not very quick to breed. I usually ensure my sows have a rest from the end of November to beginning of February and keep them on a slightly restricted diet so that they are just right for putting into the breeding pen. I cut the corn slightly but ensure a good supply of greens, roots and hay.

Most sows will breed up to about 3 years of age although some will stop before this and some will go on until they are 4 or 5, the average life span of a cavy being 3/5 years though here again some individuals will go on to 8 or 9 years. Boars seem to live longer than sows and can sire occasional litters at 5 or even older.

Care of the Pregnant Sow

The reason that it is recommended that sows be rested during the latter part of the winter is because litters due in the months of January and February put a strain on sows, this being a time of the year when stock are at their lowest ebb. Food is beginning to deteriorate due to long storage, the weather and general factors of winter can cause stress, and losses of breeding stock are at their highest at this time of year.

The most one can do if litters are due during these months, or indeed at any time of the year, is to ensure that there are no undue problems in the caviary. Cavies are essentially timid animals very susceptible to stress which is known to be the cause of more deaths and abortions than any other factor. When buying mated sows it is wise not to buy one that is more than 4 weeks pregnant. When you bring your mated sow or your new stock home, allow them to settle down as quietly as possible, do not handle them immediately, follow the diet the breeder has recommended to you, and keep all cats, dogs, birds, and even children out of the caviary. Undue noise, sudden movements, or unaccustomed activity can cause a strange cavy to become very upset at breeding time.

Feeding the pregnant sow during the winter months must be given some thought because she must not be allowed to become fat but at the same time must eat enough to provide for her own needs and those of her unborn babies. Do not be lavish with corn, particularly during the last three weeks of pregnancy. A small handful of crushed oats one day and a small handful of bran mash the next day is quite sufficient. Plenty of really good hay is important, as much as she can eat and enough to busy herself about in as well as to keep her warm. A daily supply of fresh Vitamin C bearing foods should always be available because her requirements are doubled to 20 mg per day during pregnancy. As the Vitamin C content in roots is diminishing during the winter try to provide some form of greenfood each day in addition to roots. The extra trouble of finding just a little is well worth it when the litter finally arrives.

Difficulties Giving Birth

Most sows can give birth quite easily to surprisingly large

babies, although sometimes with a first litter there may be a dead one. If there is only one baby which is large it may die during birth if this is prolonged. However, when difficulties do arise there is quite a lot that can be done to help either by a vet or by an experienced breeder. Luckily it is not often that assistance is required as the cavy is a very good mother and can do all that is necessary herself.

If a sow is straining to give birth, particularly if she has already delivered one baby and no more babies appear after 15 minutes, then it is obvious that she will need some assistance. A baby may be coming with its head bent either backwards or underneath or it may be coming hind feet first. If there is nothing showing outside the sow, then it is necessary to make an internal examination. Have a clean towel and some vaseline handy, then gently lift the sow onto your lap supporting her heavy tummy. Place a little vaseline on your little finger and gently slide it into the sow. This will not cause any discomfort and is quite easily done if the rear end of the sow is just on the edge of your knee. If there is a baby inside you will be able to feel it quite plainly, if not your finger will slide quite easily for about 40 mm ($1\frac{1}{2}$ inches) into her. Usually the obstructing baby is just the other side of the pelvic girdle which you will feel just inside the sow. If a baby is coming hind feet first this is called a breach birth. If it is coming head first this is normal. If it is a big baby or one with its head presented not quite straight you will have to very gently slide your finger around to see if you can find the mouth of it. You will feel the sharp teeth quite easily so try to hook your fingernail under the top teeth and gently pull and ease the baby down and out. Keeping your nail hooked under the teeth is not easy and if you lose your grip the baby will slip back again. Once you get part of the head to the outside it is easier to keep the finger nail hooked under the teeth and not let go. Get hold of the head with a dry cloth and ease it out gently and slowly in a slightly downward curving motion. Do not pull in an upward motion. Once the head is out the rest will follow more easily, but if it is an unusually large baby care must be taken when getting the shoulders through. Try to slide it out very gently, ease the outer rim of the sow's vulva slightly inwards if possible.

Break the membrane around the baby's face so that it can breathe if it is not already broken and then put baby and the sow back in the pen. The mother will usually start licking and cleaning the baby immediately and give birth quite normally to any more babies she may be carrying. If, however, she will not touch it give it a good rubbing with a dry towel and break the umbilical cord hanging from the tummy. Usually the placenta is broken off, but if a large mass of dark red flesh is attached this is quite normal. The cord can be nicked with the finger nails or cut off about 20 mm ($\frac{3}{4}$ inch) from the body. Make sure the baby is warm and it will come to no harm. After the mother has recovered or given birth to further babies she will attend to it. Sometimes a baby can be rather slow in moving about after a difficult birth and its eyes stare upwards, but usually after a few hours, provided it is kept warm, it will recover.

If on internal examination of the sow only a leg can be felt then it is probably a breach birth. Try to ease the leg out by feeling around it and drawing it to the outside. Keep hold of this leg and try to find the other one; it may be necessary to put a slight pressure on the one leg to bring the other one down, but do not try to get the baby out just by the one leg as you could hurt the sow. When both legs are out take a firm hold and ease the baby out very slowly. It is a little more difficult and great care must be taken not to pull it too quickly. The sow will help by heaving. A baby born this way can often be alive, but if it has been in this position for long and the sow has been struggling to give birth it could well have drowned or suffocated. Sometimes a baby may be found in the pen with a leg bitten or its head bitten which is usually the result of the sow having difficulty giving birth and has reached underneath herself to drag the baby out. The cavy does not mutilate her young or eat them deliberately as some animals do. If a youngster is found injured, it must be put down at once. The quickest and most humane way to do this is by striking the back of the head a sharp blow by means of a blunt instrument or against the edge of something solid. This is not a nice thing to have to do and luckily it is not often necessary, but when one breeds animals one must be prepared to take the bad with the good.

The licking and cleaning of the babies stimulates the sow's contractions for the birth of the next baby and when the last baby is born any afterbirth that has not been passed will come away during the next 12 hours or so, it does not necessarily all come away at once.

Gradual changes take place in the body of the sow and the eating of the afterbirth, or most of it, stimulates chemical changes and the milk starts to flow into the milk glands. This causes the sow to want to suckle, but if the sow at first does not show any interest in the babies and hides in a corner give her something interesting to eat, dry the babies off, and make sure that they are warm. If there is more than one baby they usually keep one another warm, but a single baby could become chilled if the weather is particularly cold so it is best to take it into the house until the sow starts to move about, at which time it can be returned to her and she will soon start fussing over it.

Sometimes a young sow with her first litter will act as if she is frightened of them, particularly if she has had a bit of trouble. She will take a look, snort, and run to the farthest corner of the pen. I have found that hanging a cloth over the pen to keep it dark and leaving some interesting food near the babies usually results in the sow adjusting, becoming broody, and starting to take an interest. Once she starts licking them you know she will be all right. The odd ones can be a bit temperamental but even these settle down and make very good mothers once they have recovered from giving birth.

Fostering and Feeding of Babies

Large litters can be split up and given to sows that have only one or two babies for most cavies will happily foster babies. Usually this is most successfully done when the babies are only a few days old as it can be a little more difficult when the foster mother's babies are older than the other babies, the younger ones may get pushed out when it is feeding time. A sow with only one baby makes an ideal foster mother. Rub some of the damp litter from the foster mother around the baby and if the sow starts licking and fussing over it then you can be sure she will accept and feed it. However, if she will not accept it she will keep pushing it away, grind her teeth, and may even make a snatch at the baby, although sows do not usually hurt them. In such cases the baby will have to be returned to its original mother who will not mind the smell of the other sow's litter and will soon clean up the youngster. If a baby is not getting enough milk it usually gets a 'tucked up" look over the hips and hind legs. As the new fancier progresses he will recognise this look and be able to ensure that the particular baby is fed extra milk by means of an eye dropper for a few days until it can fight its way to the milk with the others.

If a mother should die and you are left with a litter that you cannot foster, then they can be hand reared. Sherley's Lactol or similar milk powder can be obtained from chemists and most pet shops, and 1 teaspoonful of this mixed with a little warm milk to a creamy consistency that will run through an eye dropper should be fed every two hours for the first day or so. Ideally this should be through the night also, but one feed would do at night. The babies soon become adept at sucking at the dropper, but do not squeeze the milk into their mouths or they will choke; let them take it at their own pace, about one eye dropper full each at first and increase it to whatever they will take. In addition to this always put some of the mixture mashed with a little brown bread in a shallow dish so that they can get accustomed to helping themselves. Once they do this keep the dish clean and freshly filled each day and stop the feeding by eye dropper except for perhaps the smaller or slower ones. You will have to clean the babies up around the face and mouth as their mother would normally do this. They will, in addition to the milk, require exactly the same food as an adult cavy, but for the first few days it is wise to mince up the carrot and beetroot, unless of course it is summer and you can find some succulent grass for them. The time and effort spent in hand rearing is well rewarded by the sense of achievement it gives you, particularly if one turns out in the end to be a big winner or a pretty pet.

If a sow should lose all her babies and you do not have anyone else's babies to foster onto her, provided she is fit and well she is best put immediately back into the breeding pen. This prevents her moping around looking for the babies she has lost as some become quite upset and rush about turning their feeding pots over and crying and squealing whilst some will just sit and sulk and not eat for a couple of days.

Luckily the foregoing troubles are the exception, but sooner or later you may encounter one of these in a sow that will need your immediate assistance, and if you know what to do you really can help.

Babies are usually fed by the mother for about four weeks and they should then be separated into the different sexes. The young sows can be left with their mother a little longer if she is not being put into the breeding pen and provided she is not tired of the babies. Sows will show this by chasing them away, in which case remove them completely.

The young sows can be put with other young sows of similar age, but some chasing and aggressiveness may be shown resulting in ears being torn, so it is well to watch them carefully. Oil of sassafras, Mentholatum or Vick lightly smeared on the hand and rubbed over the fur, particularly around the rump and under the chin of the newcomers and the ones already in the pen, may detract from the new smells and encourage them to agree together. However, any aggressive ones or any that appear timid and frightened and do not mix with the others are best removed if they have not settled down after a couple of hours.

Weaner boars will agree very well together from different litters. A lot of activity will ensue at first by way of chasing one another, but this is mainly showing off and exercising of aggressive feelings titillated by the new smell. Do not worry if your young boars for the first hour or so seem to be indulging in rather sexual behaviour, they soon settle down and forage about together in the hay. They will agree quite well for ranging periods, but at about 3 months old they start becoming aggressive, chattering their teeth which is a sign of attack, and then they will bite rumps and tear ears and should be separated before this happens.

An adult boar will tolerate a young weaner boar as company and this is very handy if you just have one baby boar with no companion. Smear one of the recommended nice smelly ointments on both of them and usually you will find that the young boar is more precocious than the older one. Provided the older boar does not grind his teeth, they will settle down in an hour or so and become the best of friends. Of course, you must not do this if the older boar is in the company of sows and the weaner boar should be removed once he is approaching breeding age. When running young boars together never put any hay or feeding pots in their pen that have been anywhere near sows or they will discover the new smell and start to fight over it very quickly. Provided they are kept well away from sows they will live quite happily together for some time.

Sexing

Sexing young cavies can be a bit of a problem until you are used to doing this, when they are older the difference is quite obvious. They are, however, quite similar whilst very young. The male will show a tiny round, slightly raised protrusion about the size of a pin head with a tiny dot in the centre, and very slight gentle pressure in front of this will usually result in

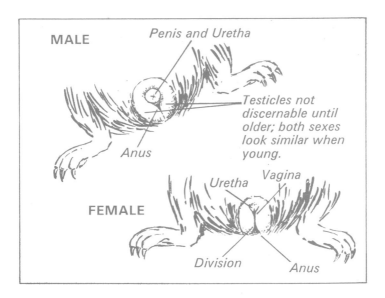

MALE

Penis and Uretha

Testicles not discernable until older; both sexes look similar when young.

Anus

FEMALE

Uretha

Vagina

Division

Anus

the tiny penis showing slightly, but do not press or poke around the area. The female looks very similar but instead of a tiny round opening from which she urinates it is slightly elongated, more like a tiny slit, and below this the division of the vagina and the anal opening may show slightly as a tiny pink blob of flesh, but again do not poke or prod about the area. The foregoing diagram may give some indication, but close examination of an actual cavy will show a slight difference and practice will soon make it quite easy. Young boars will usually demonstrate their sex even whilst with their mother by walking on their toes and weaving their bodies about and making a familiar purring noise. If a young weaner is put with a strange young cavy it will quickly demonstrate if it is male or female, the male will behave as previously described but a young female will just look around or look rather timid. Only adopt this method if you cannot determine their sex by the former method as your youngster could be severely told off by the strange cavy. The first minute or so should give you an indication before any aggression sets in.

Young cavies should be handled with care as they are inclined to jump about and can even jump right out of the pen if a good deep drop board is not used. When handling them they should be handled as the adults with the hand underneath the belly and the hind legs not able to get a foothold, thus preventing them from jumping. Both hands should be employed for handling youngsters, one supporting and the other over the top of them. They will throw themselves right out of your hands if care is not taken and severely injure or kill themselves.

Breeding Records

If you are keeping and breeding cavies with showing in mind, records should be kept of each animal that you intend to breed or show. On this record should be entered details of their own breeding if this is obtainable from your original supplier, details of the animal's markings or make-up, its date of birth and, if you keep more than one breed, its breed and from what strain or breeder it came.

Keeping details of their litters and what they have produced and what similar characteristics they appear to pass on to their offspring when mated to different animals is also recommended. These details can in future generations often prove helpful, especially when mating related animals together, or be helpful in showing that it would **not** be wise to mate certain individuals together because of inherited characteristics that you do not want to increase in your stock.

If the animal is a show cavy or a potential one then records of its progress, its placings at shows, comments on points that any particular Judge seemed to prefer, the competition, and so on, can again prove to be quite helpful in the future, particularly if showing again under the same Judge.

Some studs have cards placed on the pens on which details are entered, but these are inclined to become marked or lost. A ledger kept in the caviary or some files in the house where one can sit in comfort and write up the details is the method I prefer. An example of the record sheet I use, which I rule up on several sheets of paper with some carbons between is shown overleaf.

It will be seen that there is a section where the date when the cavy will be 5 months old can be entered. This ensures that when entering a youngster for showing I know at a glance how long it is eligible for the Under 5 Month Classes.

SIRE : _____

DAM : _____

GRD. SIRE _____ Male Side

GRD. DAM _____ Male Side

GRD. SIRE _____ Sow's Side

GRD. DAM _____ Sow's Side

NAME _____

SEX : _____ BORN _____

5 mths old on : _____

STRAIN : _____

BREED : _____

MARKING ETC. _____

SHOWING DETAILS

BREEDING DETAILS

42

CHAPTER FOUR

The Self Varieties

A "Self" Cavy is an animal that is the same colour all over and is smooth coated. The same standard applies to all the breeds of self cavies and the allocation of points is identical, the only difference being in the requirements of colour.

Self Breeds (or varieties)

Short, smooth haired self coloured

Self Black
Self White
Self Cream
Self Golden
Self Beige
Self Lilac
Self Red
Self Chocolate

As can be appreciated, colour is a very important part of the Self's makeup. Many have good top colour but it is not always carried right down to the skin. Texture of coat must be soft and silky, not harsh and coarse. In both cases breeding and careful grooming are the only ways to achieve this.

Type is another very important factor and this includes the shape of the head and the body. The makeup of the head should be bold, broad and blunt, the sow having the better type than the boar. The body should be cobby and square and the shoulders deep and broad. As we go through the breeds it will be seen that some self breeds excel more on some points than on others.

Eyes must be big and bold, not small and deep set or fatty. This latter condition is a problem to the self breeder seen when the lower lid falls away from the eye and a white/yellow fatty lump develops. The ears should be large and drooping, not standing to attention. Condition is most important in the appearance of the Self cavy and although only 10 points are given for this, the difference between a fit animal and an unfit one is so obvious that no matter how good the type and colour if it is not fit it cannot make up a loss of 10 points.

The standard for the Self cavy is as follows:

Colour	− Deep and rich	30 points
Shape	− short, cobby body, deep broad shoulders, roman nose	25
Coat	− short and silky	15
Ears	− rose shaped, set slightly drooping with good width between	10
Eyes	− large and bold	10
Condition		10
		100

The standard colour requirements will follow each breed as we go through them.

The Self Black

The Self Black Cavy is indeed beautiful, its supremacy is borne out by its continued success and popularity over many years. More than any other breed of Self it can come nearer to the standard for shape and type and colour and has taken more Best in Show awards than any other breed of cavy. Because the sow has the better shaped head and a softer coat she is the show pig; boars are a little more pointed in the face, but they must have very broad, bold heads and a really good one can sometimes beat a sow.

As much is expected of the Self Black, there is a great deal to breed for and competition is very strong; producing a real "Flyer" is no easy matter, particularly breeding them consistently which is what you have to aim for. It takes time and it takes patience, but when you see a real good one set up on a box, you will know what I mean.

Faults that must be watched for are crinkly ears or a folded hem on an ear. Some Self Blacks tend to be rather small, but a good one should have good size and substance and be of good shape, not long and narrow on the shoulder. Although the standard does not mention size, the competition is so great that the Self Black must have that something extra in order to win.

You will not go far wrong if you go to a breeder who has established a record of consistency over the years and take the advice that is given to you. Feed them well, treat them kindly and they will give you a lot of pleasure.

The standard requires the colour to be black, deep, and lustrous, the same going down to the skin. Eyes to be black.

The Self Cream

This is another breed with exceptionally good type and shape. It has deep ruby eyes which set off the cream colour to perfection. There are a number of different shades of cream, in some parts of the country the preference is for a darker and in other parts for a lighter cream. As the name suggests, it should be the colour of the cream at the top of a bottle of Jersey milk. A dark cream is inclined to be a bit strong or even brassy and too light a cream rather insipid. The main problem is undercolour which is much paler than the top colour. Whether this is due to the introduction of Self Whites in the breeding is a question on which breeders seem to differ greatly.

Evenness of colour is very necessary and this is difficult to obtain if the undercolour is too light as it will give the coat a patchy, flaky, uneven appearance.

Skill in breeding is required for the litters contain different shades of creams and you cannot just keep breeding light to light; some of the darker ones must be used to keep a good even colour throughout the stud and therefore the advice of an experienced breeder must be sought when first starting on this very attractive cavy.

The standard requires: CREAMS should be a pale even colour with under colour to match and free from lemon or yellow tinge. Eyes ruby.

The Self White

This is a very popular breed which like the Self Black has excellent type with the lovely blunt head. The Self White normally seen is the pink eyed Self White but black eyed Whites are now accepted as a standardised breed and are usually exhibited in the same class as the pink eyed.

A fine Self Black owned by the author.

A Self Cream sow owned by Mrs. M. Pearce.

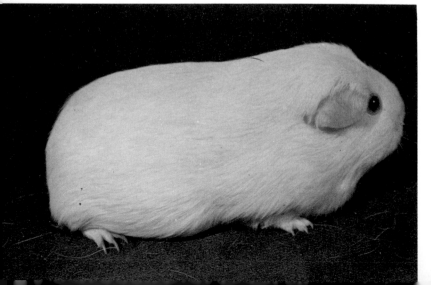

Whilst the Self White has the beautiful shape of head, it does not have the same shoulder substance as the Self Black. Ears tend to be rather small and crinkly or bend at the edges which spoils the overall appearance. This is a fault which must be carefully watched in the breeding pen as it is a very dominant fault.

It is surprising the different shades of white that can be seen in a line up of whites on the show bench, and although this breed does not have any trouble with undercolour as it is white all the way to the skin, the shades of white can vary from yellowish to greyish but the really snow white exhibit stands out. The coat must be soft and silky, some whites tend to have rather coarse coats although these are not seen as often as they once were and a great improvement has been made in this direction. The large baggy exhibits are rarely seen now, the coarseness has been bred out and the shape improved but some are inclined to be rather long and snaky. The black eyed White is also improving but pigmentation of the ears and pads of the feet has to be watched and eyes that are not truly dark but more ruby must be taken into account.

A Self Beige sow owned by Miss P. Crosse.

Self White sow owned by Mrs. M. Pearce.

The Self White must be presented for showing without a mark or stain on its coat and achieving this is far from easy. Constant attention must be paid to the bedding so that the pen never becomes dirty, thus staining the coat particularly on the underside and around the vent. When transporting them to shows the travelling boxes must be carefully wiped to ensure that no dust or dirt can mark the coat, and at the show itself it is wise to wipe thoroughly the wire pen in which the animal will be placed. This is a beautiful breed but an everyday one, not just a weekend one.

The standard requires: WHITES should be pure snow white throughout, ears and feet to match body. Eyes pink (or black).

The Self Beige

This is usually a very big, bold breed of cavy. The standard states the colour should be that of real beige cloth, but there are many shades of beige cloth. It is, therefore, a colour that will be fixed in the mind and aimed for after seeing a good coloured beige cavy. Usually the light medium coloured beige with a slightly pinkish overtone is the preferred shade. Undercolour is usually good but evenness of colour must be bred for. The eyes of this cavy are pink.

Unfortunately type is not as good as in the black, white, or cream, and it is a much longer shape. Although the boar has not quite such type as the sow it is he who is usually the show animal because he keeps his shape better than the sow who is inclined to become baggy around the belly, particularly after being bred from, although of the two she will, of course, have the better type. Different shades of beige are produced in the litters and skill is needed to select those that will blend together to produce required beige. Dark coloured animals should be used in your breeding programme, so do not discard those youngsters and keep only the lighter ones or you will find that patchy offsprings will result, some having dark lines or bars on the coat. When born youngsters are quite dark but lighten as they mature. The ears must be carefully smoothed down into a drooping position as they are inclined to have rather "fly away" ears.

They are rather long in coat and as the standard requires a short silky coat, careful attention must be paid to their show preparation for they are not easy to groom and the coat can soon become ragged and broken looking. Light coloured cavies tend to suffer from "broken back" which means breaks in the fur and scurfy skin which is usually caused by lice or the feeding of food that is high caloric. Attention to diet is essential; maize and other high calorie foods should be avoided and strict attention given to lice infestation.

The standard requires: BEIGE should resemble real beige cloth with ears and feet to match. Eyes pink.

The Self Golden
The colour of this cavy should be that of an old golden guinea, although in fact it varies from brassy yellow to almost pale red. However, once having seen a really good golden cavy the colour becomes fixed in your mind and adds up to a very pleasing animal. They have pink eyes, are usually big

bold animals, but seem to have lost the lovely type that they once had. Many today are the correct colour which goes right down to the skin but type and coat quality does not seem to have improved which is a great pity. There are still one or two breeders with Goldens of good type and it is worth trying to obtain some of their stock if you intend breeding this popular colour. Young Goldens are very dark when born and for this reason are not usually showable until older.

The colour of the feet is sometimes somewhat lighter than the body colour and this must be considered when breeding as it is a fault penalised on the show bench. Because of the different opinions as to colour it is as well to aim for type and provided the coat is even in colour right down to the skin and not brassy then you will not go far wrong.

The standard requires: GOLDENS should be a rich golden shade with no suggestion of yellow. Ears, feet, and toe nails to match body colour. Eyes pink.

The Self Lilac
This breed is another of the big bold type of self. The colour is difficult to explain and has to be seen to be fully appreciated; it can best be described as a dove grey with a pinkish

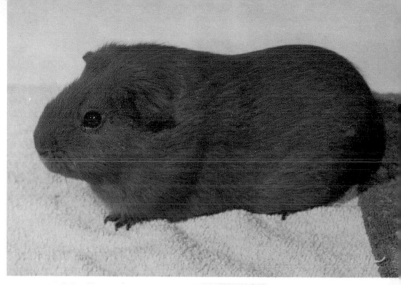

Above: Self Red Boar owned by Mr. R. Bebbington.

Opposite: Self Lilac sow owned by M. & L. Bebbington.

Below: Self Chocolate owned by Mrs. M. Pearce.

tinge. It is sometimes mistaken for Beige but when the two breeds are side by side, there is no resemblance, the lilac leans towards grey whilst the beige to fawn. Undercolour is usually no problem but grooming and preparing the coat is very important and can do a lot to improve their makeup as they are rather long coated and the texture slightly inclined to coarseness. Youngsters are very dark when born, and lighten as they grow. Barring and patchiness has to be watched as do light feet and fly away ears which can also have dark edges which must be bred out.

The standard requires: LILACS to be pale lilac carried down to the skin. Eyes pink.

The Self Red

This is one of the self breeds that is not quite so popular as it once was. It is certainly a most attractive colour, being a rich mahogany which must have a fiery look about it. The deeper shades tend to have a poorer undercolour than the lighter shade but as long as the colour is even, the under-colour good, and the whole effect has a fiery tone, not a pale colour, then that is what to aim for. The eyes should be ruby. Unfortunately type is not very good.

It is an interesting breed because the youngsters can change colour, going from dark to light and back again. Some even have a covering of white hairs which disappear leaving a good coloured coat. The show life of a young red is extremely limited due to these changes and it does better when it is in adult coat. It is certainly a cavy that is different and one with a challenge that deserves more fanciers taking an interest and trying to improve on what we have rather than trying to breed what we have not.

The standard requires: REDS should be a dark rich colour, the same going down to the skin. Feet and ears to match body colour. Eyes ruby.

Self Chocolates

Not readily kept these days which is a pity for this is one of the oldest breeds of selfs having a lovely shade and probably the softest, silkiest coat of all the self breeds. The lovely ruby eyes are most attractive. This is not the largest of the self cavies, tending to be a smaller breed and lacking type although occasionally a good typey one is seen, but very often this is due to the introduction of black blood. The skin of the Chocolate is lighter than the fur and as a result the area of the eyes and nose may appear pinkish due to the finer and shorter hairs. This also applies to the ears which should be smoothed down when young to encourage them to droop. When breeding, care should be taken that litters do not contain babies showing considerable coloured hairs as they are inclined to carry cream coloured hairs on the shoulders, and around the hips and also patches of red.

The standard requires: CHOCOLATES should be a rich dark colour with ears and feet to match body. Eyes ruby.

CHAPTER FIVE

The Non-Self Breeds

The Non-Self breeds include smooth coated, long smooth coated, and rough coated varieties, each has its own standard as accepted and approved by its own Specialist Club and the National Cavy Club.

Some breeds are quite new and were formerly under the guidance of the Rare Variety Cavy Club which caters for new or rare varieties. Although standardised, they are still under the care of the R.V.C.C. and a list of these and some of the unstandardised breeds catered for are mentioned at the end of this chapter.

Non-Self Breeds

Abyssinian	Rough, short haired	(rosetted)
Dutch	Marked, short haired	(smooth)
Himalayan	Marked, short haired	(smooth)
Tortoise and White	Marked, short haired	(smooth)
Tortoiseshell	Marked, short haired	(smooth)
Agouti	Ticked, short haired	(smooth)
Peruvian	Rough, long haired	(rosetted)
Sheltie	Smooth, long haired	(non-rosetted)
Crested	Rough, short haired	(rosetted)

The Abyssinian

The Abyssinian Cavy, or "Abby" as it is usually called is probably the most popular of the Non-Self varieties. It is an ideal breed for beginners as it does not require the show preparation necessary for other breeds like the Peruvian, the Agouti, or the Self. The Abby is a very active creature that bristles and bustles about, never happy to be still. Breeders talk a language of their own for a breed that is unique in its makeup; such things as furnishings, mane, collar, ruff, saddle, ridges, hip rosettes, and rump rosettes. The placing of the ridges is very important, if they are correct then the rosettes which come between the ridges will be straight and well placed, and in this breed only the harsher the coat the better.

At small shows the various colours are usually entered in one class but at the larger shows and particularly at the Abyssinian Stock Shows the colours are split up into different classes.

BRINDLE is an intermixing of red and black hairs
TORTOISESHELL is patching of red and black
ROAN is an intermixing of Black/Grey and White
STRAWBERRY ROAN is a mixing of Red and White
TORTOISESHELL AND WHITE is Red, Black and White markings
SELF COLOURS include Black, Red, and White, and some of the rarer markings are the Agouti and Himalayan.

The distribution and mixing of patches, roaning, or brindling has nothing to do with the requirements of the smooth coated breeds of the same name. In the Abby the patching or mixing of colour is not considered, it must merely carry the colour or colours of its respective type. However, an allowance of 5 points is made in the standard because some of the colours can be poor, a black should be black not a rusty black and red should not be a faded red. Although it is said that no good Abby can be a poor colour, if two good ones were tying for first place at a show and one had a stronger colour this would be the decisive factor.

Of all the colours, the Brindle usually has the harshest coat and selfs the softest. Harshness must be bred for, it does not come from keeping them in colder atmospheres as is popularly supposed.

The main part of the body is called the Saddle. There should be four rosettes across and round the middle of the body, running around the back in an arc, one on each side and one on either side of the backbone ridge. Further back over the hips are another four rosettes, one on each rump and one on each hip forming an arc over the back quarters. All the rosettes should be deep and start from a pin point centre. Poor ridges will make rosettes look flat and will be penalised. Rosettes on the rump are inclined to run in what is called guttering or channelling, and sometimes a rosette will be a split or double rosette. The ridges divide the rosettes and should be stiff and upright, not flat. The ruff or collar ridge goes around the shoulders behind the ears. The main ridge runs between the ears and down the centre of the back. Flatness of this, particularly the section from the ears to the ruff, or mane, is quite common in otherwise good exhibits due to shortness of coat. Flatness of this ridge behind the ruff is often due to shortness of coat and lack of shoulder substance. The upstanding ruff, mane, and moustaches or furnishings are immediately noticeable when you first look at a good specimen and they give the crisp bristling appearance.

When purchasing a trio of Abbys, the boar should be the one of highest quality and as near the standard as possible. A double rosette is not such a bad fault as flatness of ridges, rosettes, or missing rosettes. The sows should also be good but slight faults are acceptable, indeed all cavies have some fault, perfection being that which we all strive to achieve.

Because of his sex the boar will have the harsher coat and is usually the show pig. For this reason it is very wise to keep a number of good boars, do not make the mistake of relying on just one and do not attempt to breed and show the same boar. If you show your boar frequently he may go sterile, as showing can upset him. If you keep a number of boars you can show occasionally and breed frequently from each one.

When babies are born they will show their rosettes, ridges, and furnishings, but these are inclined to go quite flat after a day or so and indeed almost disappear, returning again around weaning time.

It is particularly important to keep your stock free of lice because they can cause the rosette centres to become open and scurfy and the hair to fall out. Heating foods such as maize should not be fed as this could also cause the same trouble.

The standard for all colours is:

Rosettes	20 points
Ridges	20
Coat (this refers to harshness)	20

Shape and size	10
Head, Furnishings and Mane	15
Colour	5
Eyes and Ears	5
Condition	5
	100

Agoutis

Golden and Silver are the two main colours, but Chocolate, Cinnamon, Lemon, and Salmon are occasionally seen. Agoutis are generally big, bold, and very fit animals with a bright, glossy appearance. The Golden should be a rich mahogany colour interspersed with black ticking and having a narrow golden strip up its belly. The chest, legs and feet are ticked as the body. The colouration of the Agouti is only at the hair ends and does not go down to the skin.

The Silver has a narrow silver/grey strip up the belly whilst the rest of the body, head, chest, legs, and feet are silver/grey evenly ticked with black.

Evenness of ticking is of prime importance and this should extend to the feet, on which many fail by being too dark. Shading and patchiness can occur and is to be penalised.

Silver Agoutis differ from the Goldens when breeding as they sometimes have what are called "dilutes" in the litters. These are non-ticked cavies that look somewhat like a self black. Dilutes are useful in the breeding pen to darken colour when silver to silver matings are producing stock that is too light. Dilute to dilute is not recommended.

Different shades of Silver and Golden are produced and some are useful in producing the desired show colour. When purchasing your initial stock your supplier will give you some pointers on this subject. Ask him to show you how to groom out the long guard hairs, a show requirement.

When breeding the following are prime faults to watch for:

Eye circles. This is where the ticking does not go right up to the rim of the eye, only the main body colour which makes the eye appear to have a light circle of colour around it.

Excessive white hairs in the body, white toenails, uneven ticking, dark feet, side whiskers, light chests and chins are faults. Special attention must be given to colour.

The standard for all Agoutis is:

Silver Agouti Boar owned by Mr. R. Reay.

Colour	20 points
Evenness of ticking throughout	30
Shape	20
Eyes – large and bold	5
Ears – well shaped and drooping slightly	5
Size combined with quality	5
Coat and Condition	<u>15</u>
	100

The Dutch Cavy

This breed carries its points on its markings which must give a balanced appearance. The distinctive white blaze and coloured cheeks give it a striking appearance which is noticeable before the rest of the animal is assessed. The coloured cheeks should be full and round but not so full as to go under the chin and must not take in the whisker bed, but go as near as possible without touching and yet not go so far back as to extend past the cheek bone.

The white blaze should be wedge shaped running to a point between the ears and the neck which is white and should be clean (this expression means free of colour and the line clear cut).

Dutch come in many colours, but the red are the most popular and the better marked ones seem to come in this colour. Blacks are the next most popular. Other colours are Golden Agouti, Silver Agouti, Chocolate, and Cream. Whatever the colour, the ears must be the same colour as the body; if the ears carry white this is called "flesh ear" and is penalised. It is possible for a well marked Dutch to win with a partly flesh ear, but it is a fault which should be carefully watched in the breeding pen.

Where the colour of the body joins the white it should be as clean cut a circle around the body as possible, the top part being called the saddle and the underpart being called the undercut. The colour should go down the hindlegs to a point about 15 mm (half an inch) from the toes, known as the stops, which should be white and equal on each hind leg.

Faults encountered are skew saddles and saddles lying back, often referred to as a slipping saddle. A Dutch Cavy

Black Dutch Cavy owned by Mr. J. Tenner.

should be BALANCED and this is the main point to keep in mind when breeding. A pair of cheeks that are either a bit light or a bit heavy but both the same are better than one correct and the other one odd. A pair of stops, even if they are rather long and are then referred to as stockings (but they should not extend beyond the hock), are better than one the correct length and the other too short or too long as this does not give a balanced effect. Even if the stops are so short as to cover only the toes, provided they are balanced and the toe nails are also white, this again is balanced.

This evenness or balance is difficult to achieve and one must be dedicated and prepared to take many disappointments, but you have as good a chance as the next Dutch fancier of breeding a good one.

The standard for the Dutch in all colours is:

Blaze and Cheeks	15 points
Clean neck	10
Saddle	10
Undercut	10
Feet Stops	15
Ears	15
Eyes	5
Colour	10
Size, Shape and Condition	10
	100

The Tortoiseshell and White

Usually referred to as the Tort and White. This is a breed for the sportsman and it is surprising how often breeders of Dutch are also breeders of Tort and Whites. They are sportsmen because the gamble of producing one near the standard is to some extent a matter of luck, though years of dedication to line and clean patches free from brindling must play a major part in producing these highly attractive, but often exasperating animals. It is a bright, dazzling animal displaying its three colours of red, black and white brilliantly contrasting in squares or patches up one side and down the other in a different colour sequence.

It is seldom that one is bred really near the very exacting standard, but the clarity and clear cut lines of some of the squares has to be seen to be appreciated. Others have their colours in patches rather than squares, but they too are most attractive.

It is important that the colours are good, the red must be deep not ginger or brassy looking, the white dazzling, and the black jet.

The aim is to get the three colours alternatively patched up one side with a dividing line up the middle of the back and to repeat the patched effect down the other side but in a different sequence, the same going under the belly to a line up the middle. There are a number of combinations of the three main colours and the patches can be more than three, but too many patches do not give quite such a distinctive appearance as the three clear and distinct colours.

The standard calls for a head that is half one colour and half one of the other colours, running in sequence with the other patches. This is extremely difficult to obtain and many Tort and Whites have the familiar white wedge of the Dutch marking with the rest of the face black or red.

The main faults to watch for are brindling and belts of colour or bands of colour. There are many ways to breed for Tort and Whites, but in all cases clear patching is the main goal to aim for and these animals are selected for breeding. You can breed only from the best you have and try to improve and use those that have patching or plenty of colour about them well distributed. It is so seldom that one is bred that can conform to the standard, but anything that comes anywhere near the standard is able to be shown. Although as previously mentioned dedication to lines and patches must be the main object when breeding, it has been found that the two most unlikely mismarked mates can produce quite a good specimen, probably because there has been a continuity in their own breeding and whilst not correct themselves they have passed on their inherent qualities.

The standard for the Tortoise and White is:

Patches to be clean cut, clear and distinct	25 points
Equal distribution and uniform placing of patches	25
Colour	20
Shape and size	15

Tortoiseshell and White showing markings on right and left sides owned by Mr. J. Tenner.

Eyes and ears	5
Coat and condition	10
	100

Faults: Cavies being short of any coloured patches on either side shall be penalised.

Side whiskers: A tuft of hair standing out just behind the jowl.

Band: A patch of colour going round the body.

Belt: A patch of colour going part way round the body.

The Himalayan

This is an interesting breed because its extremities are dark and its body colour white. The babies are born white and the pigment on the legs begins to show through in a few days although the fur is not completely dark until about 5 to 6 months old. The two colours seen in this breed are Black and Chocolate. The Black is not as dark as the Self Black, but the nearer to this the better. The Chocolates are a milk chocolate shade. The body on both should ideally be white, but this is very hard to achieve together with really dark points. The darker the points the harder to get a really white coat. Many are creamy rather than white and some are very muddy in colour and inclined to be patchy.

Breeders usually refer to this breed as "Hims". The dark nose is called the "Smut" and should be quite large and extend up the nose between the eyes, and lower down should spread into the whiskers. The smut is worth the most points individually so the larger and denser this is, the better. The ears should be a matching colour, of good shape and drooping, not standing up in the air. The feet or "the points" as they are called must be dense and the colour go well up the leg but not beyond the hock.

The show life of the Him is rather restricted as young ones under five months do not have the dense points which are not usually fully through, being interspersed with white hairs which disappear as the animal approaches 5 to 6 months of age. Adults start to lose density and the white hairs again begin to appear as they age. The density can also change from day to day and it is said that a knock or injury can cause the colour to temporarily go white.

63

To prevent poor coloured blacks being shown as chocolates there is a separate standard for each. Dark shades of chocolate are heavily penalised.

The body colour does not carry a large proportion of points and it is quite possible to do very well with a darker body colour than is called for if the smut and points are particularly good. When you have seen a really light body colour together with really dense points and smut, you will not be satisfied until you too have bred the ideal.

The standard for the Black Himalayan is:

Nose – even and jet black	25 points
Feet – jet black	20
Ears – shapely and jet black	10
Coat and colour – short and silky and pure white	20
Size and shape	10
Eyes – large, bold ruby red	5
Condition	10
	100

The standard for the Chocolate is:

Nose – Even and rich milk chocolate	25 points
Feet – rich milk chocolate	20
Ears – shapely, rich milk chocolate	10
Coat and colour – short silky and pure white	20
Size and shape	10
Eyes – large and bold, ruby red	5
Condition	10
	100

Peruvian

This is the long haired member of the Cavy family. An adult in full show coat is a superb sight and a credit not only to careful breeding but also to the patience and perseverence of the owner who must be prepared to brush and rearrange the long hair every day. More care and attention must be lavished on the Peruvian than any other breed. It is a full time occupation to breed and show Peruvians. It is not a beginner's cavy, but is one that fascinates a great many fanciers, many of whom unfortunately seem to take them to intermediate stage and then give up. This is understandable because the standard requires the hair to be soft and silky yet very dense, and the softer and silkier the coat the harder it is to keep free from tangles.

Not all Peruvians have the temperament to sit still on their special show boards when being judged, or waiting to be judged at a show. They have to do this so as not to spoil their long coats which can grow up to 50 cm (20 in) or more. It is reckoned the coat grows 25 mm (1 in) in a month and the longer the coat grows the more likely it is to break and become thin at the ends. The animal itself can undo in seconds the work of months, by tangling its hair, losing a wrapper which keeps the hair bound up, or by chewing a piece of hair, so a great deal of thought must go into the decision to breed Peruvians for showing.

Anyone contemplating this breed is advised to join the Peruvian Cavy Club which will give information on the Do's

Black and White Peruvian with coat brushed out owned by Mrs. P. Wood.

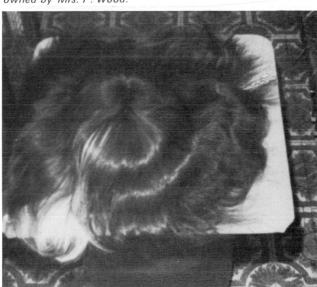

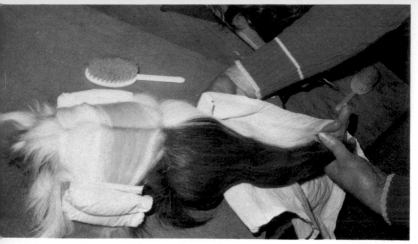

Tri-colour Peruvian.

and Don'ts as it would take nearly a book in itself to go into the requirements of the Peruvian for show purposes.

Peruvians that are used for breeding must have their long coats cut off and cut very short around the back end and around the genitals, in order that they can mate. The coat should be cut short regularly so that the animal can move about with ease and not become entangled in its own fur. During the summer the coats are cut as short as possible so that the animal does not suffer from heat exhaustion. Show animals with their long coats and wrappers should be kept in a well ventilated position in the caviary to be kept as cool as possible in the extremely hot weather. In the winter, of course, the coat serves as a very good means of keeping the cavy warm and can be allowed to grow down to its feet on breeding stock.

When Peruvians are born they are short coated and should have two rosettes sited on the rump, but the hair does not grow towards the rump but towards the ears, the opposite direction to the other breeds, only the hair below the rosettes grows downwards. As the animal matures the hair will start to part up the middle and should be encouraged downwards on each side of the parting. Eventually the hair is brushed over the two rosettes into what is called the sweep and when long enough, at about 3 months old, it is taken up into what is called a wrapper made of paper and a small piece of balsa wood and secured with a rubber band. At about $5\frac{1}{2}/6$ months of age the side hair is put into side wrappers, one on each side, and this is where problems can start as these are inclined to come out rather easily, though when the hair becomes longer they do stay in better. If the wrappers are not put in with great care they can cause the animal to chew itself. Provided the wrappers are comfortable and the animal is given sufficient hay which must be cut into lengths of about 75 mm (3 in) and pressed well down to stop the cavy from burrowing underneath it, chewing should not occur, boredom is probably the cause of this because show Peruvians must be kept on their own. Lice can also cause irritation which will make a Peruvian scratch its fur out.

The hair over the Peruvian's face is called the frontal fringe and this is probably the hardest to breed for. Many lack on frontal, and it is also the most difficult part to keep long and dense and the most likely part to become chewed. It can be seen therefore that the Peruvian fancier has a challenge before him that depends not quite so much on breeding but on his own tenacity.

The standard for all Peruvians, which come in a variety of colours and combination of colours is:

Head — broad with prominent eyes	5 points
Fringe, with hair completely covering the face	15
Shoulders and sides	15
Texture to be of a silky nature	20
Density	15
Sweep, length and fullness, the hair falling over the hindquarters	15
Condition	5
Size	5
Presentation	5
	100

The hair should be fine, silky, and glossy.

The fringe should be furnished so that the hair hangs in a thick mane on each side of the head.

The face should be short and the eyes large and full.

While we aim for a straight coat, a slight wave should not be unduly penalised.

If the sweep is slightly longer than the sides, this does not constitute uneven length.

Young Peruvians are very large for their age, much bigger than even some of the Self breeds. Their age is usually determined when being shown by the length of their coat and therefore taking into account that it usually grows at 25 mm (1 in) a month the top hair will give an indication of the age.

The Sheltie

This is one of the new breeds of cavy and was accepted as a Standardised Breed in 1973. It is a long haired breed rather like the Peruvian, but the hair grows differently. It has a smooth face and the hair from the head grows down like a mane which is carried along the body to join a sweep like the Peruvian. The Sheltie does not have the hip rosettes of the Peruvian. The head of the Sheltie should be blunt, not pointed. They are an easier breed to manage than the Peruvian as they require only one wrapper to keep the sweep in order. They have no middle parting, the hair is swept back over the body just falling around the shoulders like a cloak. They do not have a fringe hiding their faces and this is part of their appeal, their pretty faces can be seen when they are set up on their special show board. As with the Peruvian they must have the temperament to sit still and be shown and are trained to do this as babies.

The Sheltie is a mutation from the Peruvian Cavy and was under the guidance of the Rare Variety Cavy Club until it was accepted by the National Cavy Club as a Standardised Breed eligible to compete in open breed classes. It now has its own club called the Sheltie Cavy Club with a growing membership of enthusiastic breeders.

Type, texture, and density are very important and the colours are varied and very attractive.

The standard for the Sheltie is:

| Head | — Broad with short nose and large prominent eyes with hair lying towards the rump | 10 points |
| Mane | — Sweeping back to join with sweep and is not parted | 15 |

Shoulders	— Broad with hair slightly longer continuing along the sides at equal length	20
Coat	— Silky texture and good wealth of coat at sides	20
Sweep	— Length and fullness of hair falling over hindquarters (sweep generally to be longer than sides which should be even in length	20
Size	—	5
Condition and Presentation		10
		100

All colours and mixings of colours are acceptable. White is the hardest to keep as staining around the rear end can spoil for showing.

The Crested Cavy

This is a new breed accepted by the National Cavy Club but formerly under the guidance of the Rare Variety Cavy Club. This is a variation on the Self Cavy but cannot be called a Self because it is not smooth, it has a rosette which is placed between the eyes and ears. It is called the English Crested Cavy because in England it is allowed to have the crest or rosette the same colour as the body colour whilst in America it is only accepted if it has a white crest on a coloured body

Moja – the first ever Lilac Crested at eight months owned by Miss McLellan-Sim.

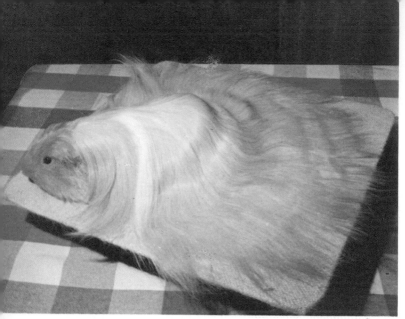

A Sheltie — one of the new breeds owned by Mrs. Lawson-Reay.

A pair of Crested cavies owned by Miss McLellan-Sim.

or a contrasting crest to the body colour.

The standard for English Crested Cavies is:

Crest	— To match body colour	20 points
Colour	— To conform to the colours of the matching English Self	24
Shape	— Short cobby body, deep broad shoulders	20
Coat	— Short and silky	12
Ears	— Rose petal shaped, set slightly drooping with good width between	8
Eyes	— Large and bold	8
Condition		8
		100

The crest to radiate from a centre point between the eyes and ears. The crest to be a deep rosette, the lower edge to be well down the nose. Any different coloured hairs in the crest to be severely penalised. Abundance of different coloured hairs on body to be penalised as in self cavies.

The American Crested must have a crest contrasting to the body colour. The crest colour to be as near to a complete circle of solid colour as possible. A circle of less than 75% to be severely penalised. The crest colour should not appear elsewhere on the body. A blaze of the crest colour to be severely penalised. Hair of body colour in the crest to be penalised. Although this American Crested is extremely attractive, it is also extremely difficult to breed with just the colour contrast in the crest.

Himalayan Crested and Agouti Crested Cavies are also making their appearance and their standards are given by the Crested Cavy Club.

RARE VARIETIES

Although some of the cavies about to be mentioned are Standardised and accepted as breeds they are regarded as Rare Varieties because they are bred by only a few fanciers and come under the guidance of the Rare Variety Cavy Club.

The Tortoiseshell

This breed is rarely seen now although it is a very old variety. Probably the Tortoiseshell and White has overtaken it.

71

The main problem is brindling and breeding them without any white patches. As with the Tort and White the patches are alternated and reversed on the other side.

The standard for the Tortoiseshell is:

The standard is:

Patches clear and distinct	45 points
Eyes large and bold	10
Coat	10
Size shape and condition	20
Colour—Black and Red	15
	100

The above standard also applies to the Bi-colour except that the standard states the Bi-colour to be marked in the same way as the Tortoiseshell but in combinations of any two colours other than black and red.

The Tri-colour—the same standard applies but states "The patchwork consists of three self colours and when one of the colours is Agouti then it is known as a Harlequin." The Harlequin is not standardised however. Where the three colours are referred to they should not be a combination of red, black and white which is the colour of the established breed of Tortoiseshell and White which has a different standard. Tri-colours are usually Chocolate, Cream and White.

The Roan

The smooth roan is a breed that is under the guidance of the Rare Varieties Cavy Club, but will probably form its own Specialist Club in due course. This breed quickly became popular and is accepted by the National Cavy Club as a Standardised Breed.

It should be an even mixture of black and white hairs free from white or black patches. The head and the feet to be black. This cavy is a made variety from originally mating Blue Roan Abyssinians to Self Blacks.

The standard for the Roan is:

Roan mixing – to be even throughout	45 points
Head and feet – solid black	15
Eyes – to match body colour	10
Colour and Coat – silky coat and colour black and white	10

Ears – black and slightly drooping	10
Size, type and condition	10
	100

The Smooth Brindle

This is a breed with few followers today except for one or two stalwarts. It is an attractive breed made up of red and black hairs evenly intermixed. As with the Tortoiseshell you seem to get brindling where you want patching, with the Brindle you get patches where you want brindling. It is a challenge to anyone wanting to breed something different.

The standard for the Smooth Brindle is:

Evenness of brindling	45 points
Eyes – large and bold	10
Coat – short and silky	10
Size, shape and condition	20
Colour – black and red	15
	100

Although this breed is standardised and accepted by the National Cavy Club it is still under the guidance of the Rare Variety Cavy Club.

UNSTANDARDISED BREEDS

Under the guidance of the Rare Varieties Cavy Club

These breeds can only be entered in Rare Variety Classes and Unstandardised Classes and cannot compete against Standardised Breeds. They are still in their development stage and will be considered for standards by the Standards Committee when it is thought they have reached that stage of development to warrant it.

The Dalmatian: A mutation from the Self Black. Basically a white body with black/grey spotting, dark legs, dark head with white wedge up the nose and ruby eyes. A Provisional Standard for guidance only. Full Standard imminent. This cavy was introduced at the Rare Variety Stock Show by the Author.

The Dappled Roan: Found in litters of Dalmatians, the roaning is uneven and hence the name Dappled.

Saffron: Originally from Self Goldens, a yellowish version of this breed.

Dark Eyed Golden: As the Self Golden but with dark eyes.

Strawberry Roan: Produced by mating Self Goldens to Strawberry Roan Abyssinians.
Sable: A shaded cavy.
Rex: A mutation that has appeared once or twice in this country and in America, the coat seems to grow differently to any other breed but not like the coat of the rex rabbit.
Harlequin: Previously mentioned with Tri-colours.

Opposite: A beautiful Sheltie cavy with a few of its cups and rosettes won for its owner Miss McLellan-Sim.

A Self Lilac.

CHAPTER SIX

Showing

The basic requirements of showing a cavy are that it is fit, clean, and well presented. Fitness comes with good management and feeding. Cleanliness includes not only giving the cavy a bath but also ensuring that its nails, eyes, and nose are clean, not stained with droppings, food, or dust, and it is very important that it is free from lice. Well presented means ensuring that the toe nails are not too long, that the general appearance is clean, sparkling and where the standard calls for it the coat is groomed short or in the long haired varieties that the coat is not knotted or tangled.

A bath given a week before a show will improve the condition of the coat and remove the grease that accumulates, particularly on boars, as well as help to remove the scurf caused by natural skin debris. However, some of the lighter breeds may need to be washed nearer the show, but generally to give the coat time to settle down and resume its sheen a week is usual. Peruvians and Shelties, for whom density is one of the main requirements, are bathed about 14 days before a show to allow the coat to resume its natural density. If bathed only a few days before the show the coat texture may feel finer but the density will not be as good.

Bathing a cavy is not difficult and the animal usually shows no objection or fright if it is handled carefully and with consideration. A plastic washing up bowl in the kitchen sink is the easiest way. First place a dry cloth on the draining board, this is to lift the cavy onto to give it a good lathering and also between changes of rinsing water. Fill the bowl about half full with warm water, ensure it is not too warm and that any hot water cannot drip onto the animal from the hotwater tap or heater. Take the cavy on the palm of the hand and gently lower its back legs into the water. Gradually let it get the feel of the warmth and sit it in the water up to about its middle, still keeping the hand firmly underneath it and supporting its front legs on your wrist. Do not let it sit in the water unsupported, or it will panic. With your other hand gently saturate the coat, a small cup can be used to pour the water over the shoulders and back. Do not get any water beyond the ears or on the face unless it is a light coloured cavy and the face and head requires washing, in which case this is best done by gently rubbing the fur clean with a cloth, avoiding the eyes. Take some ordinary hair shampoo and work it into the coat with plenty of water. You can if you wish lift the cavy out onto the dry cloth on the draining board to work up a good lather, but still keep your hand supporting the animal as there is nothing more slippery than a soapy cavy. It should then be rinsed, the lathering repeated and rinsed three or four times until all traces of soap are gone. A boar will often be particularly greasy and to remove the grease a good quality dish detergent used as a shampoo will help. Particular attention should be given to the grease gland that is at the base of the spine but do not rub so hard that you make the animal's skin sore, it is better to bathe a couple of times if necessary to remove the grease. Always use warm water for rinsing and then wrap the cavy in a towel, take it into a warm room, and gently rub it as dry as possible, particularly under the chest and around the hind quarters. If you have a hand hair dryer or a small fan heater which can be set to warm heat this will help to dry the fur quite well and cavies do not seem to mind this at all, some will stretch out quite happily until they are dry. If you keep long haired cavies a hand hair dryer is essential as the wrappers must not be put in until the fur is absolutely dry, and the quicker you can get the long hair dry the less likely it is to become damaged by the cavy stepping on it. It is wise when drying a long haired one to do this in sections. Wrap up the wet sides in a cloth wrapper and dry the sweep, then put the wrapper in the sweep and do the side sections separately until completely dry. This will prevent the cavy stepping on its coat or trying to dry itself and chew the fur.

A fan heater is satisfactory provided it is not of the type the cavy could jump onto and get its feet caught in the louvred opening or jump onto the revolving fan or heating element.

Before the cavy can go outside to its own pen it must be thoroughly dry, and if the temperature of the shed is very much lower than the drying room it is best left overnight in a box in the house with plenty of warm hay and some food, and returned to the shed the next day. The risk of pneumonia could mean the loss of a good cavy. In the warm summer, provided there is no direct draught and the cavy is quite dry it will come to no harm being put out when it is dry if it is given plenty of hay to keep it warm and clean.

Any brush used for the coat should be a soft bristle brush, not a stiff nylon one. For the self breeds a shoe brush of soft texture is ideal and will remove any dust or scurf that may gather between bathing and showing.

When the standard calls for a short silky coat the long guard hairs must be groomed out and this is best started well in advance of the show, doing a little each day. Starting at the rump, lifting the coat between the thumb and forefinger, you will see there are very long coarse hairs overlaying the shorter coat. These long guard hairs must be rolled or teased out of the coat, gradually working over the animal until an even finish is obtained. It is not, however, quite as simple as that for this is one procedure which cannot adequately be described on paper, it requires a practical demonstration and usually a self breeder at a show will oblige the newcomer. At first it does seem a tedious job and it takes a lot of practice to do it correctly, but when it is done it makes all the difference to a coat, giving it a short silky finish, and in a close contest at a show the difference between 1st and 2nd with two animals of equal merit. After seeing an ungroomed cavy and a groomed one the look and the feel of the coat will be apparent. However, a word of warning, until you have mastered the art do not practice on your best cavies, but rather on ones that you do not intend to show for you could ruin a show animal for several weeks by overgrooming or breaking the texture of the coat.

If a cavy is intended to be a show animal then it must be handled regularly and taught to sit quietly when it is put down. To get an animal accustomed to this routine it is a good idea to groom it in your house where it will become used to different surroundings, to being handled, to noise, to sudden and unexpected movements, and to being carried about. It is surprising how quickly they can learn, particularly if taught when young. A well behaved animal will sit quietly when being judged and not be jumping about all over the place with stewards and Judge trying to calm it down. It will show itself off to its best advantage if it sits naturally and not poking its nose skywards. You can teach your stock to be "little showmen".

All breeds of cavies have a Specialist Club which caters for their members. They hold Stock Shows throughout the country, usually an Adult Stock Show and a Young Stock Show. The Self breeds are catered for by the English Self Cavy Club, usually referred to as the E.S.C.C., and each of the Non-Self Breeds has its own Specialist Club. Any unstandardised or new varieties and a couple of rare standardised breeds come under the Rare Varieties Cavy Club, referred to as the R.V.C.C.

The Scottish National Cavy Club caters for the Scottish Fanciers and covers all varieties, and shows are usually held under their Rules in Scotland. The South of England has the Southern Cavy Club which again caters for all breeds and has its own rules and regulations under which its shows are held.

The National Cavy Club referred to as the N.C.C., is recognised as the main Cavy Club and the Parent Society to all Specialist Clubs, and is open to all breeds. Shows in general are run under National Cavy Club Rules unless otherwise stated on the schedule, and as there are one or two differences in the rules of various clubs make sure before you enter your cavies that you are not likely to infringe one of these rules unintentionally. The club relevant to your area will send you a copy of their rules when you join and send your subscription—do read them. Club secretaries are always pleased to help with your queries and a self addressed envelope is always helpful.

There are also many area and local cavy clubs that organise shows at regular intervals. Shows are advertised well in advance in the small livestock magazine called *Fur and*

Feather obtainable by order from newsagents or by subscription from *Fur and Feather* of Idle, Bradford, Yorkshire. It is published fortnightly and contains information on forthcoming shows and reports on shows held, naming the winners. Stock for sale and wanted together with articles written by breeders are other useful features of the magazine.

You may exhibit at shows without becoming a member with the only exception being the rarely seen Members Only Shows. However, if a Cup Show or any trophies are offered then if you are not a member you will not usually be eligible for these should you win, although rosettes and ribbons are usually given to non members if they are offered in the schedule. Any special awards offered by specialist clubs are only available to members of those respective clubs. In order to claim a Championship Certificate it is necessary to be a member of your specialist club and a member of the National Cavy Club and any other Club that will recognise your Championship Claim, each club having its own ruling about Championships.

Unless the schedule is printed in the Show advertisement and this usually only applies to the very big shows, in order to compete you must write to the Secretary whose name and address is given and ask for a show schedule, stating that it is for the Cavy Section, as Secretaries also deal with rabbits and other small livestock. If there is a special Cavy Secretary the advert will state this. Always enclose a stamped addressed envelope for your reply as most clubs rarely show much profit and expenses have to be kept to a minimum. When you receive the schedule you will see that it is divided into two Sections, the Self Classes and the Non-Self Classes. Depending upon your breed of cavy it should be entered first into its breed class, if your particular breed is not mentioned then it will be classed under either the Self Any Other Colour, shown as Self A.O.C., or if it is a Non-Self it will go in the Non-Self Any Other Variety, shown as Non-Self A.O.V. You will then see that there are classes called duplicates, sometimes these classes will just have the letter "D" and the class number. You cannot enter into these classes alone, you must first either enter your breed class and then enter the duplicate classes. In the duplicate classes you will be competing against other breeds. Usually after each class there will be a further one for the young pigs shown as under 5 months which means the animal must be *under* five months of age.

Only Standardised breeds accepted by the English Self Cavy Club and the National Cavy Club can be entered in classes called A.O.V. or A.O.C. If there is no class listed as Rare Variety or Rare Variety Unstandardised then an Unstandardised cavy cannot be entered. If there is a class then your cavy can only be entered in that class and cannot be duplicated. Unstandardised cavies cannot compete against standardised varieties.

Usually schedules are for Adult cavies and Under 5 month cavies but some shows also have a section for Intermediates which are just out of the under five month age group but not yet 8 months old. It is referred to as the 5/8 months Class and should you enter for this then you cannot also enter an adult class. When there are no intermediate classes you may enter the adult classes once the animal is 5 months, but this is usually a disadvantage as most animals do not have the maturity at that age to compete with adults, although some of the marked breeds can do very well as youngsters. You are not obliged to enter in all the classes and may enter in your breed class only, although it does help the club if exhibitors duplicate into the other classes, and if you feel that your animal is worth showing why not let it come up against some of the other breeds.

Some of the abbreviations used in show schedules are as follows:

Ad. Adult	S. Sow
U/5. Under 5 months	AC. Any Colour
5/8. 5 to 8 months or Intermediate	AOC. Any Other Colour
A.A. Any Age	AV. Any Variety
B. Boar	AOV. Any Other Variety

Breeders. You must have bred the cavy yourself. If you bought an in-pig sow and she had her litter in your caviary then her babies would be considered as bred by you and you could enter the Breeders Class. You cannot enter the Breeders with an animal you have bought and not bred yourself.

Juvenile. Means only open to Juvenile exhibitors. The term Juvenile differs slightly regarding age limits, so reference must be made to the Club about this.

Novice. Unless otherwise stated means the cavy not to have won a 1st prize at any show. If it is stated that the exhibitor is to be a Novice then the exhibitor must never have won a 1st prize at any Show.

Pet Class. This is usually for Juveniles only unless otherwise stated. Crossbreds or pure breds can be entered. They are judged on cleanliness and fitness only and cannot be entered into any other class.

When you have filled in the entry form and worked out how much your entry fees are it is usual to send a postal order or cheque with your entry to the Show Secretary to arrive before the date on which entries close which is usually stated in the advertisement, although sometimes entries are accepted up to the time of showing. It is always a help to the club if you can send your entries in advance so that the necessary book work can be completed and thus save extra work on the day.

When the day of the show arrives the cavy should be taken to the show in a special carrying box which is divided into sections. This is easy to make if you are a handyman but can also be purchased ready made, usually at the shows. Quite often in *Fur and Feather* carrying boxes are advertised, but do not purchase rabbit boxes which are too large for cavies. The compartments should not be so large that the cavy can be thrown about whilst being carried, nor so small that the animal is cramped and cannot turn around comfortably. You should ensure that there is plenty of ventilation and that the animal cannot get over the top of the divisions into the next compartment when the lid is closed. Place some sawdust or shavings in the bottom of the box and some hay cut into lengths of about 100 mm (4 in) for the cavy to nibble and to keep it clean. It is wise to take with you to the show a little extra sawdust and cut hay in a bag. Take with you some food to keep the animal occupied, but in the case of light coloured cavies nothing that will stain the coat or the mouth. You will also need to take your grooming brush and a soft, silky cloth to give your cavy a last brush and rub before placing in the show pen. Peruvians and Shelties will require the special boards on which they must be shown. Rules for these boards are given by the Peruvian Cavy Club.

When you arrive at the show, you must report to the Secretary or whoever is booking in the cavies and tell him your name. He will tell you the pen number for each animal to be exhibited and will give you a label for each on which will be written the pen number. The label should be stuck onto the cavy's ear before you put it into its respective pen which will bear a corresponding number. Sometimes the labels are stuck on when the stewards take the animals to the Judge and you just put your animal in the pen number allocated to you, but the former is the usual method. Should any ear labels come off they are replaced by the stewards at the judging table. The ear labels cause no discomfort and are placed on the top of the ear so that the number can be seen.

Peruvians or Shelties usually have the ear label stuck on their special show board thus preventing the sticky label becoming entangled in the long hair. You must make sure that you put the correct pig in the correct pen or you might find your boar coming up in the sow class or your Under 5 month exhibit being shown in the adult class.

Usually it is made quite clear to you when receiving numbers which label is for which pig. Before putting your label on it is wise to prepare your pen. Sometimes there is sawdust already in the pens, but a good thick layer is required and this is where your own supply comes in useful. Spread it out into the corners of the pen, thus ensuring that it will soak up the urine which could stain the coat or make the animal wet underneath. Many animals go up to the Judge sopping wet underneath due to insufficient sawdust in the pen, and all the work of preparation has been spoilt. On top of the sawdust place sufficient hay for the animal to busy itself about in, but not so much that the stewards cannot find the animal.

The show pens have often been stored since last being

used at a show and could be dusty or dirty, so give them a good wipe around with a tissue or piece of old cloth. It is wise to ensure that the door fastens correctly and that the divisions between the pens are secure and there are no gaps at the back through which the animal could escape or trap itself in. Ensure that it cannot get its head or feet caught underneath the pen. When you are quite satisfied that all is secure and clean you can give your cavy a brush and wipe with the cloth, place the label on one of its ears, and place it carefully in the pen. If you are showing an Abyssinian then you cannot brush it, but a soft toothbrush can be used to tease up the ridges and remove any dust or sawdust that may be in the rosettes. Peruvians and Shelties go into their pens with their wrappers in, but it is as well to check these to see that they have not loosened with travelling. The rest is then up to the stewards and the Judge. The stewards take the cavies from their pens to the table for judging, and they then return them when the Judge requests them to do so.

Mr. A. E. Roebuck judging Dutch Cavies.

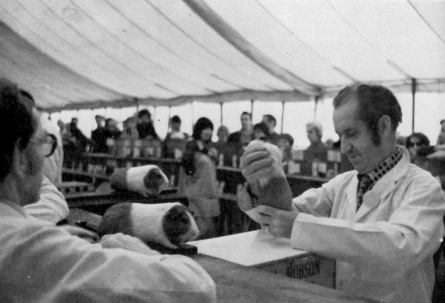

Exhibitors of Peruvians or Shelties are allowed to take their own animals to the Judge due to the fact that the animal must be placed on its show board, its wrappers removed, and its long coat brushed out and arranged to its best advantage. The cavy must not move but sit quite still on its board even when being carried to the Judge. Before the Peruvian Class is to be judged, the stewards usually request those showing these or Shelties to begin preparing their animals and to be ready when the Judge calls them. There is usually a table set aside upon which the fanciers prepare their stock. If you are exhibiting one of these breeds you take your exhibit to the table, tell the Judge or the book-steward your pen number, the sex of the cavy, and the colour or colours, and that is all you need to say. Have your brush ready in case the Judge wishes to re-arrange the coat. If your animal does move and its coat become disarranged ask permission of the Judge to re-present your cavy. Though rules vary in different parts of the country, and brushing your cavy at the Judging table is not allowed by many clubs, generally if there is room you will be allowed to go to the end of the table and do this. Just what is required will soon be learnt and what you can and cannot do will be apparent.

Exhibitors should on no account indicate or try to indicate to the Judge which is their cavy, nor should they, if asked to help with the stewarding, make remarks about any of the cavies or intimate which cavy on the table is theirs, or point out faults on other exhibits in the earshot of the Judge. Although a Judge will ignore such remarks other exhibitors will not and will be rather displeased, so be careful not to make yourself unpopular by improper behaviour at a show.

The Judge has a book in which are entered all the numbers of the cavies in each class; he does not have a list of names of exhibitors and will not know until after the show to whom each animal belongs. As each class is presented he will spend a few minutes assessing each animal, and if he has a book steward the steward will write his comments against each cavy or the Judge may prefer to do his own book and write his own comments alongside each animal. When he comes to the duplicate classes, he may not always call for all the animals entered, as once having handled them in their breed classes he will have his notes and the animals he will want to consider will usually only be the principal ones that have won or been placed in the breed classes. He will compare these against each other, but any cavy that has not been placed will usually not be required.

Eventually the Best Self exhibit and the Best Non-Self exhibit are chosen, and there is usually a Best in Show which will be one of these two. However, it should be remembered that Best in Show is not a class which is entered, nor is it always the winning adult in the Grand Challenge. The animal which the Judge considers Best in Show may be an animal which has only been entered in one class, its breed class, or only part way through the schedule, but if he considers that this animal comes up to its standard better than any other exhibit, he can appoint this Best in Show. Sometimes an Under 5 month or an 5/8 month cavy is awarded Best in Show if the Judge considers it is a better representative for its age than the adult cavy is for its age. The only requirement of a cavy that becomes Best in Show is that it must not be placed above any animal that has already beaten it in any class. If it has not met any exhibits other than those in its breed class simply because it has not been duplicated, this will all be taken into consideration and compared before the final decision is made.

Prize money is shown on the schedule either as guaranteed prize money, in which it is guaranteed that a certain amount is paid for every 1st, 2nd and 3rd prize, or it can be on a 75% basis. This means that 75% of the entry fees are put back as prize money, the other 25% being used by the club to cover expenses. The amount of prize money then depends upon the number of exhibits in each class.

The schedule will usually state when stock can be removed after judging. You cannot take your cavy home after it has been judged even if it has not been placed. Each exhibit makes up part of the show whether winning or not and people come to the shows to see the cavies and are entitled to see all the entries. Most shows have very good refreshment facilities and you will meet many new friends and learn lots of interesting tips.

After a visit to a show everything will seem much clearer

and you will generally find that fanciers are only too ready to help a newcomer, but do give the other exhibitors time to get their cavies into their pens and sort themselves out first before asking questions. Once they have put their stock in their pens and the show is under way you will find them ready to talk and swap hints.

When the Judge has finished judging you are quite at liberty to have a word with him, and indeed to ask him what he thought of your cavy and to point out to you its good points and what to try to improve on.

You can ask to be shown how to groom out the guard hairs of your cavy if it is the type that should be groomed short. If you are a Peruvian or a Sheltie breeder you can watch how the experienced fanciers put the wrappers in, the size of the wrappers, and pick up lots of hints on preparation. It will also give you a chance to compare other cavies with your own and to see what is required in any particular breed.

It is certainly not unknown for a new fancier to do extremely well at a show the first time, so never feel that you or your cavy are not good enough to come up against the more experienced fancier and because of this hesitate to show your own stock. Do remember, however, that one win does not make you a ready made expert. You may go to another show under a different Judge and with different competition, or even the same competition, and not do quite so well. Consistency is what you have to aim for. Breed your own winners, do not buy them in at big prices; stockmanship is what counts, not showmanship. What you have in the breeding pen is what makes your stud even more than what you have on the show bench. No matter how long you may be in the Fancy you will always learn something you did not know, always be ready to help and always be ready to listen and learn. Win well and lose gracefully and then you will be a fancier.

CHAPTER SEVEN

General Management and First Aid

When picking up cavies great care should be taken that the weight of the body is well supported. Never pick them up by their shoulders. Apart from frightening the cavy by restricting its lung cavity by pressure on the ribs, the lower heavy part of its body could twist and cause internal damage. The correct method is to slide your hand, palm upwards, underneath the belly, your fingers going between the hind legs.

The correct way to hold a Cavy is illustrated by the author.

The legs should hang loose on either side (see photograph) as in this way they cannot get a foothold to use as leverage. The front feet and chest should rest on your wrist, the other hand being placed over the shoulders to steady the animal. Never carry more than one cavy at any time in your hands.

When putting the cavy down again just lower the hand and slide it from underneath. Because of its bulky build and very short legs a cavy is not made for jumping, the hind legs have very little muscle, and if it is allowed to jump from any height, even about 150 mm (6 in) it could damage its shoulders. The cavy will hurl itself off if it is frightened or even just adventurous. If a cavy should fall it will usually land on its nose, not on its feet. On no account should it be allowed to jump down from boxes or chairs or from your knee, this could result in broken or misplaced bones or even worse.

Cavies soon become accustomed to being handled, and as can be seen from the photograph this young black sow looks quite happy being held up for the camera. She has been handled from birth with showing in mind and will not struggle or fidget when she is shown for the first time and the Judge handles her.

Properly looked after the cavy is generally a healthy animal, but occasionally some treatment may be necessary and knowing what to use and what not to use can save suffering to the animal and loss to yourself. Do not hesitate to seek the assistance of a vet should you have any doubt as to the problem or the treatment.

Lice

Although not an ailment, it is more of a pest, cavies do carry lice, but let me hasten to add that these lice do not live on humans and are rather different in that they usually only live on skin debris. However, if you intend to show your cavies, they must be free of lice.

Because the cavy is very susceptible to many drugs and antibiotics one must be extremely careful of any preparation that is used either as medication or insecticide. Flea and louse powders recommended for dogs and other animals are not always suitable for cavies.

An old fashioned remedy that is very safe and effective is

Oil of Sassafras which is not obtainable generally but is available through Herbalists, Health Food Stores, and some chemists.

If a cavy is carrying lice it will have small white specks around the rump which can be seen when the hair is divided and sometimes the eggs can be seen at the ends of the hair. Oil of Sassafras will kill the lice and remove the eggs, which other preparations will not. A small amount of oil is required and it must not be used near the cavy's eyes. If there are any eggs in the cheeks then great care must be taken in applying the oil in order that it does not come into contact with the eyes, and when working over the back of the cavy, ensure that none comes into contact with the genital regions. Remember that a little of this oil goes a long way and the animal does not need to be smothered. When putting the animal back in its pen include plenty of hay. The oil soon evaporates and in a few days leaves the fur in a nice glossy condition. This treatment should be repeated in 14 days and again in a further 14 days to ensure that the cavy is completely free. Once the cavies are free of lice, it is probably only necessary to ensure that fresh stock do not bring in lice or that none are picked up at shows. A general treatment once every couple of months will keep the cavies lice free.

Mites

In recent years there seems to have been an increase in a mite infestation called "Sellnick" which causes a mange-like condition which is extremely painful and distressing to the cavy. It is caused by the mite which burrows into the skin but it is too small to be seen by the human eye and incidentally is not transmittable to humans. This condition is seen mostly around the neck and shoulders and spreads from there. The hair comes out, the skin is scurfy, and eruptions appear that are sore and open. The animal will lose condition and cry with pain, and because of the stress which it can cause the animal can die. A pregnant sow will almost certainly abort her litter if affected. Treatment must be given immediately and the recommended treatment is Tetmosol which is used for the treatment of scabies in humans. The cavy is dipped in a solution of **1 part** Tetmosol to **72 parts** of warm water. **Do not** use according to the label on the bottle as this is the human usage. Simply dip the animal into the solution, making sure that the sore or scurfy parts are covered, do NOT rinse off. Gently dry the animal with a towel and dry off with a hand held hair dryer. When completely dry return it to its pen which should have been thoroughly cleaned out and washed with a solution of Tetmosol. Any other animals must also be bathed in Tetmosol also to prevent it spreading. This treatment should be repeated in 14 days time and in a further 14 days time. Once the first treatment has been completed the animal will improve and the hair will soon grow again.

If you do find any cavies with sores or bare patches do not use Oil of Sassafras, but suspect Sellnick and use the Tetmosol, which will remove lice anyway. Tetmosol liquid is obtainable from chemists who will usually order it for you if they do not have it in stock. Pet shops generally have only Tetmosol soap which can be used, but whereas the liquid solution does not need to be rinsed off, the soap must be rinsed away and may, therefore, not be quite so effective for this particular form of trouble.

Eye Injuries: Cavies like to run about and burrow in the hay and often if the hay is coarse they can injure their eyes. The eyelid will be very swollen and the eye itself may become cloudy. Usually a piece of hay or a hayseed has become lodged in the fleshy membrane inside the eyelid. If it is not visible treat the eye with Aureomycin eye ointment obtainable from your vet, or some Albucid Eye Ointment that your doctor may have recommended for your own eyes. This will help to ease the eye and bring down the hay or hayseed if it is still in the eye, so that it can be gently removed. The eye will need to be treated twice a day until the cloudiness has disappeared which usually take about 7/10 days. It is not unusual in a litter of new born babies to find one with a completely cloudy eye which can soon be cleared up by using one of the recommended ointments applied three times daily until clear, just a very tiny amount is necessary.

Allergy: This is more apparent in the summer and pollen or dust is the usual cause. The eyes run and a very simple and effective treatment is $\frac{1}{2}$ teaspoonful of common salt to $\frac{1}{2}$ pint of cooled boiled water kept in a clean bottle and applied to the eye by means of an eye dropper three times a day. If the trouble does not clear up after seven days then it is not an allergy and something similar to Betsolan Eye Drops from the vet should clear this up. Do NOT use Betsolan Eye Drops on any eye injuries.

Overgrown Toe Nails: The nails of some cavies never require cutting whilst others require frequent trimming, particularly on the front feet where they can grow right round and into or under the foot. In a light coloured cavy it is easy to see how far to cut the claw as the pink "quick" is visible, but on a darker coloured cavy it is more difficult, so trim off only a little at a time until the nail looks a comfortable length. If you should cut too far and the nail bleeds dip the claw into some Evans Dermal Powder obtainable from chemists. Nail clippers of the type that look like very small wire cutters are the best kind to use. If you should not have any E.D.P. handy unperfumed talcum powder will do, but best not cut too far as it is rather painful for the cavy.

Overgrown Teeth or Breaking of Teeth: Sometimes a cavy will break its front incisor teeth due to a fall or chewing the wire. They will grow again quite quickly as the cavy is a rodent, but until they do if the break is uneven they should be trimmed to an even length with nail clippers. If, however, the teeth have broken off completely or are loose in the socket then the animal will have to be fed soft foods for a few days until they begin to grow again. As long as you watch to see if it can chew things like grass or hay it will be alright but if not bread and milk and damp bran mash, both with Vitamin C added, grated carrots, and beetroot should be given plus anything else it can manage.

If an animal starts to lose weight or appears to want to eat but cannot then the teeth should be looked at to see that they have not overgrown. The front incisor teeth are very long, but if they overlap a lot they should be trimmed. If they seem to be alright then it is probably the back teeth overgrown across the tongue, and unfortunately there is not much that can be done about this which is a hereditary fault. However, if the animal is a pet the vet may be able to cut the teeth, but they will only grow over again and as the teeth are sited so far back it is probably better that the animal be put down.

However, the advice of your vet should be sought.

Torn Ears or cuts through fighting: The mother some-times tears an ear on a baby with her claws if something frightens her and she dashes over them. These chipped ears are unavoidable but of course rather spoil an animal for showing. When a number of youngsters are run together there should be plenty of feeding pots so that ears are not bitten by others trying to get at the food. Cavies sometimes fight when first put together and young boars will bite the rumps and ears of their companions but if so they should be separated. A solution of salt and water of the strength recommended for the eyes can be used for washing any cuts or scratches, and should they fill with pus they can be squeezed out and then E.D.P. powder applied.

Abcesses: These can be caused by knocks or thistles in the hay and occasionally through fighting. A fairly hard lump will be felt usually around the throat or cheek, and it is best to leave it alone. If it is an abcess it will gradually grow to quite a large size and will become softer when it is getting near to bursting point. The animal should be removed from the others and put in a pen on its own, because if the abcess does burst the others will lick it and become infected. When it bursts a lot of unpleasant smelling matter will come out. Wipe this gently away and wash with the salt and water solution, repeating each day until all matter is removed.

Magnesium Sulphate: Ointment can be applied to help draw the abcess. It may look rather alarming and quite a large hole in the flesh can often be seen. It will heal from the inside upwards, and provided it is kept clean will soon clear up. Abcesses are very seldom fatal unless they interfere with eating or breathing, and treatment by antibiotics is not recommended for cavies.

Sometimes a hard lump can be felt in the throat area and after a short time start to shrink and finally disappear com-pletely. This is probably something to do with the lymph gland. Do not prod or poke or squeeze any swellings as this could irritate the condition.

Ruttling: This is a rough sounding noise made when the cavy is breathing. As long as the animal is fit and well and eating normally it is probably what is popularly called Beetroot Ruttle, but I do not think Beetroot have anything to do with it. It is usually encountered during the winter when ventilation is perhaps not as good as it should be and the animals are being fed dryer food than usual, and particularly if the hay is dusty. The membranes at the back of the nasal passages and the throat become inflamed and cause this rasping noise. The cure is quite effective, one teaspoonful of Sulphamezathine to one teaspoonful of water per day per adult cavy. Divide this into three parts and give three doses daily. After five days the ruttle should begin to disappear but continue the treatment for a further four days on half the above dosage. Do not however treat a pregnant sow but let her ruttle along until she has given birth and weaned her litter. If it is just an ordinary ruttle she will be fine but ensure that the hay is dust free.

Scabs at the corner of the Mouth: Can be caused by animals chewing wire, but otherwise the cause is not really known. A hard crusty lump on one or both sides of the cavy's mouth will appear. *Panalog* Ointment from your vet will soon clear this up. Apply only a tiny smear to each scab twice a day. If the animal is a pregnant sow seek your vet's advice before using it on her, pregnant sows being very susceptible.

Compaction of the Rectum: This is a condition which appears in boars particularly when they are getting on in years. What happens is that the droppings compact in the rectum and form a blockage. A boar with this trouble will be found to have a large hard lump of compacted droppings and will look unusually large around the testicles. Vaseline should be eased around the lump and a dry cloth or tissue used to try and remove it either in a piece or in pieces until it is cleared. It is rather evil smelling when removed, but after this the cavy can be kept clear by regular attention and continue to live a happy active life.

Scouring: This is usually caused by faulty diet as mentioned in chapter on feeding. For this kind of scouring the animal should be put on its own and not fed any roots or greens, only hay and bran dampened slightly with water to which Vitamin C has been added. Redoxon effervescent Vitamin C tablets are ideal but one table is 1 gramme which is sufficient for 100 cavies, so break off a very small piece for one animal.

Also give water. If Shepherd's Purse or bramble leaves are available these can be given but no other form of greens until the droppings are normal. Give the animal Sulphamezathine at the dosage recommended for ruttling, and when the scouring has cleared up bring the animal back onto its normal diet and introduce greens slowly.

Enteritis is a fatal form of scouring and by the time it is apparent is often too late to treat successfully. Care should be taken not to feed musty hay, stale corn, or mouldy pellets. Roots should be carefully examined to see they are not soft or rotten. Stale food left lying in the pen can cause serious troubles, particularly mash that has gone sour and therefore feeding pots should be kept clean and washed.

Keeping cavies is really just lots of common sense, cleanliness, and attention to details. I would suggest that a First Aid Box is always kept in the caviary and the contents should include:

1 pair rounded end tweezers
1 pair nail clippers
1 tube of Aureomycin Eye Ointment
1 bottle Sulphamezathine
Tetmosol Liquid
Oil of Sassafras
E.D.P. powder

Index